LOVE

and

GOODNESS

God, You, and Helping Others

Be the reason someone smiles.
Be the reason someone feels loved.
Be the reason someone believes
in the goodness in people.

ROY T. BENNETT

MICHAEL L. NELSON

Ballast Books, LLC
www.ballastbooks.com

ISBN: 978-1-966786-57-3

Printed in the United States of America

Published by Ballast Books
www.ballastbooks.com

For more information, bulk orders, appearances, or speaking requests, please email: info@ballastbooks.com

TABLE OF CONTENTS

Please Note
There is a love and goodness example
at the end of each chapter.

THE PREMISE OF THIS BOOK

We are given a life and put on this earth to help God improve the lives of others, and in so doing, to make the world a better place. Just *believing* in God is not enough. We must also be *doing* things that help others in some way.

God works in the world through people like you and me to improve lives and improve the world. Unfortunately, fewer people are following God's guidance these days. As a result, life is becoming a more challenging experience for almost everyone.

This book focuses on the need for people everywhere to awaken to the presence of God's love in their lives and, as a result, to increase the helpful words and meaningful deeds they share with others.

What good is it, my brothers and sisters, if someone claims to have faith but has no deeds? Suppose a brother or a sister is without adequate clothes or food. If one of you says to them, "Go in peace; keep warm and well fed," but does nothing about their needs, what good is it? In the same way, faith by itself, if not accompanied by deeds, is dead.

James 2:14–17

GOD AT WORK IN MY LIFE

Our only legitimate end in life is to finish God's work, to bring
to full growth the capacities and talents implanted in us.

ERIC HOFFER

For many years, I didn't pay much attention to the fact that God was at work in my life. Nevertheless, God was signaling me to write at an early age. In my younger days, well over sixty years ago, my teachers noted not only my writing skills, but what I wrote about as well. One teacher wrote a note at the top of one of my papers that said, "Michael, you have some very deep thoughts for a young man your age."

If I could have read this book right after receiving that note, I might have devoted a larger portion of my life to putting my thoughts down on paper. Instead, I headed off into the technology world, first working for IBM for almost ten years and then developing a couple of entrepreneurial ventures with some friends of mine. But God never gives up on us. I'm certainly proof of that, now having written my fourth book after the age of sixty-five.

My first three books are about the importance of our choices. I now believe that God let me live through over sixty years of real-life experiences and several mistakes of my own to prepare me to write those three books. I was about to write another book about choices when I felt this "love signal" to focus more on God at work in our lives as it was happening to me. Very quickly, both the concept of this book and the title *Love and Goodness* came to me.

At that point, the Spirit of Goodness in my life nudged me to write this book and continued to nudge me for months as I worked through many drafts to get to what you see here today. In other words, this book came to be as a result of the love signals I have described herein. God provided me the love and desire to do this in my *heart*, and my Spirit of Goodness provided the motivation to work through it in my *head*. I mention these details here only to confirm to you that I have experienced the love and goodness in my life that I have described in the book.

My wish and prayer for you is that God's love will become an important and noticeable part of your life. I hope you will, in turn, share your goodness with the world by helping others in some way. My hope is that we will see the day when people *everywhere* are working together to make the world a better place for *everyone*. May God signal you in special ways as you make the choices that allow you to become an important part of this *love* and *goodness* work.

It is only with the heart that one can see rightly;
what is essential is invisible to the eye.

ANTOINE DE SAINT-EXUPERY

OPENING WORDS

Dare to reach out your hand into the darkness,
to pull another hand into the light.

NORMAN RICE

The Importance of Love and Goodness

This book is about *love* (God at work within us) and *goodness* (our response to that love). Love and goodness are the two most important ingredients in our lives. They guide us to our purpose for being here, as well as to people we can share special feelings with or help in some way. It is my hope that the words you find here will help you assess the roles that love and goodness are playing in your life.

Love and goodness have no limits. You can love and care about people who are close to you as well as individuals thousands of miles away whose names you don't even know. The sharing of goodness as you reach out and help someone connects your life to theirs in a special way. The extent of the goodness—whether it be a kind word, a nice meal, or a much-needed financial lift—is not the important thing. What's key is that you used your life to make another person's life a little better.

We all need to evaluate the amount of goodness coming from our lives. Goodness seems to be deficient, even missing, in many people these days. As a result, the world is becoming a more troubled place. I hope this book will motivate you to increase the amount of love and goodness coming from your life, and in so doing, make the world a better place for everyone.

God's Love Signals

I have experienced God's influence and direction in my life for a long time, but especially so in recent years. Writing this book is one example of God directing my life in a specific way. In the book, I refer to such directions from God as *love signals* that motivate us to say and do good and helpful things for others as well as for ourselves. God's love signals help us make important choices and manage our lives in more effective ways.

I believe God is with us regardless of the unwise things we may have done or the poor choices we may have made along the way. You can confirm God's presence in your life by paying closer attention to the love signals that influence you in good and positive ways. It's left to you, however, to make the choices needed to follow where God's love signals are leading you.

Although we accomplish it in many different ways, our basic purpose for being here is to help God improve people's lives and make the world a little better. God's love signals are important in helping us accomplish this task. However, it's what we *say* and *do* in response to those signals that determines the difference between a special life and an average to poor one.

Our Spirit of Goodness

To help us live in a goodness-oriented way, I believe God instills a "spirit of goodness" in each of us at the very beginning of our lives. As explained below, this spirit is given to us not solely for our personal benefit, but for the good of others:

Now to each one the manifestation of the Spirit
is given for the common good.

I Corinthians 12:7

Our Spirit of Goodness provides a feeling of sincere concern about others and supports the reason we are here: to help people have better and more effective lives. It motivates us to be a positive and helpful person and works within us this way:

Our Spirit of Goodness is an internal motivator that nudges us to actively choose kindness, compassion, and helpfulness toward others. It helps us respond to God's love signals and creates a desire within us to do good deeds and to act with positive intentions, even when it's not convenient or expected to do so.

Please note: The effectiveness of our Spirit of Goodness is dependent on the choices we make and how we conduct ourselves each day. In other words, God pre-positions us spiritually for goodness, but it's left to you and me to make sharing our goodness an important part of our lives. If there is "a little secret" about developing our lives in a positive way, it is this: The better we are at sharing our goodness with others, the better and more meaningful our lives will be.

The interesting thing about goodness is that we benefit from sharing it as much as the people receiving it from us. It's the sharing of our goodness with others that makes our life work in an effective and fulfilling way. A life lived in a selfish way, one that shows little or no concern for others, typically ends up being an empty experience. On the other hand, the more goodness we share with others, the greater the level of satisfaction we receive from our lives.

CHAPTER 1

LET'S STOP AND THINK ABOUT THINGS

Opening Thought

A s we go through life, it's beneficial to stop now and then and think about things, especially those issues that have a significant impact on our lives. Therefore, I'm starting this book with the suggestion that we do exactly that—in this case, stopping to think more deeply about God's role in our lives.

Over the years, I've thought a lot about this question: *How does God work in our lives and in the world?* It seems to me that this is one of the more important questions we will ever have a need to answer. That's because having an answer, especially one that makes sense to us, can significantly improve the way we live our lives.

I've also been thinking about another question: *Why is the quality of life declining while crimes and conflicts are increasing in almost all parts of the world?* Clearly, people throughout the world are not as happy as they used to be, and many live day to day in fear.

There seems to be a connection between the answers to these two questions. It appears to me that the further we move away from God, unintentionally or otherwise, the more stress and difficulties we have in our personal lives as well as throughout the world.

We need a better understanding of God's role in our lives and how God can help us live in a more effective and satisfying way. We need to get our thinking straight about how God's spiritual guidance can help us have a better life and a better world.

> *The happiness of your life*
> *depends on the quality of your thinking.*
>
> MARCUS AURELIUS

Our Outside Lives and Our Inside Lives

In effect, we live two lives: our *outside* or external lives and our *inside* or internal lives. Our outside lives include what we say and do each day; our work, school, and exercise activities; and our efforts to look good to others. Our inside lives include the love we feel for those close to us, the thoughts we have that determine the choices we make, and our caring and concern for other people.

We have parents, teachers, managers, and significant others who help us with our outside lives, where most of us focus as we go about our activities each day. We tend to spend much less time working on our inside lives, as we can't see them or touch them. Therefore, it's essential for us to stop, think, and determine how well we are doing in managing our inside lives. An honest assessment in this regard can lead us to make some important improvements in the way we are living each day.

Almost every one of us needs to focus more and work more diligently on the management of our inside lives. Our inside lives, without question, are the most important, as they include our *spiritual* experiences when we communicate with God and connect more closely with God's presence in our lives. Not only can God help us improve our inside lives, but when we do so, our outside lives are improved as well.

*We do not need more national development; we need more
spiritual development.
We do not need more intellectual power; we need more
spiritual power.
We do not need more knowledge; we need more character.
We do not need more law; we need more religion.
We do not need more of the things that are seen;
we need more of the things that are unseen.*

CALVIN COOLIDGE

Our Need to Stop and Think

Many people go through life without ever giving much careful thought to God's presence and influence in their lives. I know because I was one of those individuals who, for many years, was more concerned about my career, the size of my house, and my outward success than in achieving any spiritual understanding and insight. Fortunately for me, and maybe for you as well, God never gives up on us and continues to be at work within us, helping us to live better lives.

I've attended church regularly over the past fifty-plus years and have listened to hundreds of sermons containing various explanations of where God is and what God is doing. However, like many others, I've tended to simply accept what was being said and seldom stopped to question or think through the details that were being presented.

However, since retiring, I have had the time and the opportunity to write three books: *Good Choices Good Life*, *Living by Choice*, and *Life and Choices*. As I developed these books, God's potential role in our lives popped into my thinking many times. As a result, I devoted a small part of my previous books to my view of God's role and influence in our lives.

Recently, I decided to round up my thinking about God's presence in our lives. I am devoting this book to explaining how I believe God works in the world, as well as the role our choices play in allowing God to provide guidance and direction to our lives.

3

Here are four of my long-thought-about feelings about God's presence in our lives that I have now come to believe. Hopefully, they will help you as you think about God's presence in the world and how God works in your life as well.

#1. God Guides Us Through Love

I believe that God is at work within each of us and is the sponsor of the love we feel in our lives. This can be our love for another person, our love for our family, our love for our vocation or what we want to do with our lives, our love for our country or where we live, or our caring and concern for someone we don't even know—especially those in need or down on their luck in some way. In other words, God guides and directs us through the love in our lives.

Because our feelings of love are reflections of God's presence and influence in our lives, we need to pay close attention to the signals love creates. You may not have considered the source of these feelings as such, but if you have experienced feelings of real love in your life, I believe you have felt God's presence within you. Our challenge in life is to make the personal choices needed to follow where God's love signals direct us to go.

After we have recognized that we are all undeserving
creatures who have received the love of God,
who can but respond and show it in their own life?

EDGAR F. ROMIG

#2. Our Spirit of Goodness Motivates Us to Act

As explained further in Chapter 3, I believe God has instilled in each of us a Spirit of Goodness to motivate us to be helpful as a result of the love we feel. While God is the "head coach" overseeing the development of our preferences and desires, our Spirit of Goodness is, in effect, the "offensive coordinator" that motivates us to make helpful choices and do positive things as a result of the love and concern we feel. God works through our heart and what we feel; our Spirit of Goodness works through our head and the choices we make concerning what we say and do.

The love signals in our lives are very important, but it is the action we take as a result of the feelings they create that determines the impact those love signals have on both ourselves and others. It's one thing to be concerned about the family whose home has just burned down; it's something totally different, and so much more, to pack up and deliver much-needed clothes to help them get back on their feet. For that reason, I believe our personal Spirit of Goodness is key to a successful life because it motivates us to act in support of the love signals God provides.

I also believe that God and our Spirit of Goodness are with you and me right now, no matter what we have done or how we have lived our lives. We didn't have to do anything special to earn their presence in our lives. Instead, as a result of God's abundant love, they have been part of us since the very beginning of our lives. It is up to us, however, to heed their directions and follow where they lead us to go.

> *We are not human beings having a spiritual experience.*
> *We are spiritual beings having a human experience.*

PIERRE TEILHARD DE CHARDIN

#3. Love and Goodness Are Special Life Ingredients

Love, created within us by God, and *goodness*, actions we take as a result of that love, are special life ingredients that work together to stimulate and help us improve our lives as well as the lives of others. Love and goodness are the qualities that make our lives work—and work well. The better we are at prioritizing love and goodness, the better our relationships with others will be and the happier we will be in our daily lives.

- *Love* is that feeling of caring and concern created within us by God. Such love can range from a romantic love for someone close and special to a caring or concern for an individual with certain needs whose name and history we may not even know. Love signals are the primary way God directs our lives.

- *Goodness* is the action we take as a result of the love and concern we feel. Goodness is what we say or do in response to the love God has placed or inspired within us. Goodness comes to life in the words we say or in the actions we take to show kindness or to help someone in a special way in response to God's love.

I believe the *primary objective of life is to share our love and goodness with others*. The challenge for you and me, however, is twofold: first, to be willing to acknowledge that the love we feel inside has, in fact, been given to us by God to direct our lives in some special way; and second, to be willing to make the choices required to respond to that love with helpful words and actions that make life better for others. If there is a formula for living a meaningful and successful life, love and goodness are its two key ingredients.

#4. God Works in the World Primarily Through People

I believe most of God's work in the world is accomplished through people. It's logical to me that God works in the world—feeds the hungry, heals the sick, cares for the lonely, and more—through people like you and me. God sends us love signals so that we may, in turn, share our goodness with others. Bottom line: You and I are here for a reason, to use our God-given interests, abilities, and feelings—our gifts—to help others as teachers, neighbors, physicians, builders, lawyers, painters, parents, drivers, store clerks, and in thousands of other ways. God calls each of us to fill special roles that, in turn, help people have better lives.

*God depends on us to deliver the much-needed meal to the
elderly people down the street or to write the check to the
nonprofit doing wonderful work in the community. It's up
to you and me to do God's work here on earth and, through
our words and deeds, help make other lives better.*

If you are willing to acknowledge the directions God's love signals create within you and respond to the motivation they provide, you will create a spiritual partnership with God that is fundamentally important in living a positive and effective life. This partnership will help you live in a meaningful way, as it supports you in sharing your love and goodness with people both near and far away.

God's Gifts and Our Uniqueness

Why are we so different? We have different *interests*, different *abilities*, and different *feelings* that lead us to pursue different vocations, goals, and more. After years of thinking about this, I believe God has created these differences in us so that, collectively, we are equipped to take care of each other. In other words, our differences equip us, as one great family, to help each other in distinctive but much-needed ways.

I believe our motivation to fill one of these roles is God's love at work within us, directing us to be who and what God needs us to be. In other words, our interests, abilities, and feelings about what we want to do with our lives have been given to us by God so that we are equipped not only to help each other but also to carry out God's work in the world.

God gives us these gifts—our interests, abilities, and feelings—so that we can tend to the world and make things better for the people in it. We do this in three basic ways:

- *By being respectful of other people*: being kind, caring, and concerned about the people we interact with each day.

- *By fulfilling the special calling provided for our lives* through the role, vocation, or career that our God-given gifts call us to fulfill.
- *By helping those in need in special ways*: reaching out however we can to help those in need.

God has given us a purpose for being here. It is up to each of us to listen to God's love signals, work to confirm the purpose God has for us and our life, and make the necessary choices to get us there. It's pretty special to consider that God needs you and me to help others and, in so doing, to make the world a better place for everyone.

We Are Individuals with One Thing in Common

God has done us a great favor: No two of us are exactly alike. We look different, we talk differently, we act differently, we learn differently, and yes, we believe differently. Therefore, we should treat each other as unique individuals conducting our lives in different ways. *The one common denominator we have is God and God's love at work in our lives.*

Race and gender, while grouping us in certain ways, have no bearing on our ability to use our lives to share our love and goodness with others. It's up to us individually, regardless of our personal descriptors, to choose how we will live our lives and the extent to which we'll use them to make life better for others.

This is why it's so important to pay close attention to the interests, abilities, and feelings you have—and work to develop them—as you choose what you will do with your life. The signals are there. You have to be willing to pay attention to them and make the choices needed to follow where God is leading you.

The two most important days in your life
are the day you were born
and the day you find out why.

MARK TWAIN

Example 1

A LOVE AND GOODNESS STORY

Doing More than Asked

Sometimes an opportunity to demonstrate our love and goodness appears unexpectedly. Such was the case of Bill, who made the choice to "do more than asked" when he encountered a young man needing much more than what he was asking for.

Bill was grocery shopping when he was approached by Charlie, who was sixteen at the time. Charlie said, "I'll take your groceries out to your car if you'll buy me some donuts."

After talking to him and finding out that the young man needed much more than donuts, Bill said, "Come on, I'll take you shopping."

Bill helped Charlie fill a grocery cart with much-needed items. After paying and discovering that Charlie had missed his bus, Bill took Charlie and the groceries to Charlie's house. When they went inside to put the groceries away, Bill found a near-empty refrigerator, a sparsely furnished apartment, and Charlie's sixty-one-year-old mother. She had adopted Charlie but could barely support both of them with her disability check. Bill later explained, "Their situation just tugged at my heart."

When Bill got home, he wrote about Charlie's situation on his Facebook page, and the offers to help came pouring in. Subsequently, he set up a GoFundMe page which, over a period of a few months, raised over $300,000 for Charlie and his mom. Bill was then able to buy them a small house, provide for their living expenses, and set up a college fund for Charlie.

When someone asked him about Bill, Charlie said, "Nobody ever cared the way he did." Bill is one individual who made the choice to help and changed lives in a wonderful way.

What an incredible thing Bill did. Clearly, God touched Bill's heart. His Spirit of Goodness tugged on him, and he responded in a love-and-goodness kind of way. Charlie, who was a straight-A student in spite of his difficult circumstances, really appreciated what Bill did for him and his mom. This is a great example of how God will use us if we are willing to make choices that allow us to help others in special ways.

CHAPTER 2

ACKNOWLEDGING GOD'S PRESENCE IN OUR LIVES

Opening Thought

Our basic purpose is to help carry out God's work in the world by helping others have better and more meaningful lives. However, not enough of us are fulfilling our responsibilities in this regard. This is why the quality of life is declining and why conflicts between people and countries continue to increase. We need to set our selfish ways aside and commit to helping God improve lives, not only in our families and neighborhoods, but also throughout the world.

In addition to directly influencing our lives and circumstances, God also works in partnership with people like you and me to address the needs of individuals throughout the world. It's through the love that God places in our hearts, and our responses to that love, that we determine the quality of our lives and the role we play in helping others improve their lives as well.

You don't have to shout "I believe in God!" from your rooftop. However, to improve your life and the lives of others, you have to take note of God's presence in your life and make choices to do things that enrich the lives of others and ultimately make the world a better place.

*It is now evident to all people of spiritual discernment
that healing the world's woes will not come through social
or political theory;
not through violent changes in government;
but through the still, small voice that speaks
to the conscience and the heart.*

ARTHUR J. MOORE

A Partnership with God

I believe that God gives each of us a special life. With God's blessing, that life came into being on day one, followed by our initial development in our mother's womb. Further, I believe that God instills certain interests, abilities, and feelings in each of us that develop over time and, subject to how we manage our lives, define our purpose for being here and the role we are intended to fill. I believe that our life was given to us for two important reasons: first, *to help other people* have better and more meaningful lives; and second, as a result of helping others in our own special and unique ways, *to make the world better* because we were here.

Our connection to God was established at the very beginning of our lives as a result of God's love for us. Therefore, the activation of our partnership with God starts with an acknowledgment of that connection and a recognition of God's presence in our lives. It requires a willingness to accept God's guidance and a personal commitment to devote our best efforts to doing the things God and the world need us to do. We further acknowledge this partnership by affirming it to God in our prayers and by living each day in a loving and helpful way.

God provides love signals in our hearts to help guide our lives, but God leaves it to each of us to manage the day-to-day work and activities of this partnership. Therefore, the effectiveness of our partnership with God increases or diminishes based on the quality of our choices and how we conduct our lives. For me, it's not a matter of us finding God, as God found us on day one. Instead, it's a matter of acknowledging God's presence in our lives and relying on God's guidance to help us live better lives.

Our partnership with God has an important objective: to help us confirm and live out the purpose of our lives. God *never gives up* on helping us find and confirm our purpose for helping others, regardless of any poor choices or outright mistakes we may have made along the way.

It took me over fifty years to realize that God intended me to write several helpful books, including the one you are reading now. I'm living proof that God never gives up on us and continues to work in our lives to fulfill the purpose God has for us. It's up to us, however, to make the choices that help us recognize that purpose and allow it to be fulfilled.

> *When I stand before God at the end of my life,*
> *I hope that I will not have a single bit of talent left*
> *and can say, "I used everything you gave me."*

ERMA BOMBECK

Developing/Reconfirming Your Belief in God

Developing or reconfirming your belief in God and how God works in the world requires a special effort. Coming to understand God and living under God's guidance is not an "in the moment" experience. Instead, it requires some careful thinking, along with the motivation provided by a feeling that it's time for you to confirm your beliefs about God and start using your life to help others.

You have to be willing to devote time and effort to clarifying your beliefs in God and how God works in your life. My beliefs have developed over the course of many years as the result of careful thought, common sense, and seeing God at work through others. Let me touch on those three things in the hope that they will help you confirm your beliefs as well:

- *Careful thought*: I've had lots of time and many opportunities to think about why we do what we do and how our religious beliefs (or lack of them) influence the quality of our choices. And being older than most of you, I've had more time—in church and in my daily routines—to reflect on my beliefs and how they influence my life. I didn't come to believe as I do without lots of reflection about God and how God works in our lives. Likewise, it will require some careful thought (and some sincere prayers, too) for you to confirm your beliefs and start using them to guide your life.

- *Common sense*: In practicing the *helping others* component of my beliefs, it became clear that it not only made others feel better when I lived this way, but I felt better as well. Whether it's a sincere smile when you greet someone, the financial assistance you give to the disheveled man on the street, or the time you spend visiting a friend who's going through a difficult period in their life, it makes you feel better when you help someone, whether in small or significant ways. I'll give you the opportunity to road test this helpful way of living in Chapter 6.

- *Seeing God at work through others*: I've not only felt God at work in my life but have also witnessed God at work through the lives of others. I've seen people visit shut-ins to remind them that someone cared about them. I've seen church members travel to underserved countries to build freshwater systems for the people there. I've seen doctors save lives through both their knowledge and their touch. I've seen volunteers build houses for families who had nowhere to live. I've seen so many signs of God at work *through people* in the world that it was logical for me to have faith that a higher power is influencing you, me, and others to be better people and to do our part to make the world a better place.

It is the heart of the giver
that makes the gift dear and precious.

MARTIN LUTHER

The Components of My Belief in God

While others can help you, your beliefs are something you have to work out for yourself. After many years of reading, thinking, praying, and writing, I have developed five primary components or parts of my belief in God. These include:

- *We don't have to earn God's presence in our lives*: I believe God has been with us from the very beginning of our lives. There was nothing we had to do to earn God's presence in our lives. It was God's choice, as an extension of God's abundant love, to be a part of our lives. And God remains with us regardless of the mistakes we've made or the foolish things we may have done. You don't have to join any special group or somehow qualify for God's presence in your life. God is already with you, and if you ask God to do so, God will help you live a better and more meaningful life.

- *God guides our lives through love*: I believe God guides us through love. It is through the love signals we feel within that God leads us to people we care deeply about, to the career or vocation we become motivated to pursue, to projects that help others in special ways, and to being kind and considerate of people we connect with each day. God works through our hearts, creating special feelings within us that motivate you and me to use our lives to help others in some way. I believe that God is present in people throughout the world and is working to help each one of us understand that helpful thoughts, helpful words, and helpful deeds are our most important activities in life. Such actions not only improve the lives of the recipients, but they improve our lives as well.

- *God provides a Spirit of Goodness within each of us*: I believe God provides each of us with our Spirit of Goodness to nudge us to say or do something helpful for others. God creates special feelings within us through the placement of love in our *hearts*. Our Spirit of Goodness works through our *heads* to help us make choices that convert that love into goodness—words and actions that help others. Yes, the love feelings in our lives are very important. But I'm convinced that what we actually *say* and *do* as a result of feeling those love feelings is even more so. Therefore, God provides our Spirit of Goodness to help us convert the love we feel inside into actual goodness that includes words and deeds that help or encourage others.

- *God's gifts guide the development of our lives*: God has given each of us special interests, abilities, and feelings that, when properly pursued and developed, lead us to our purpose in life. There are thousands of roles, careers, vocations, and tasks that are needed to make the world work and for us to be able to take care of each other. I believe God provides this functionality by giving us the basic interests, abilities, and feelings to fill a need and help others in special ways. As an example, I believe that God eradicated polio through the interests, abilities, and feelings God gave Dr. Jonas Salk and his medical team, who worked exceptionally hard to develop the polio vaccine. God calls each of us to fill a special role in life that makes life better for others and provides us with the capabilities to fulfill those roles.

- *God doesn't force us to do things; we have choices*: God doesn't force us to do anything but instead allows us to make the choices that ultimately define our lives. God is always with us and at work in our lives. However, God leaves it to us to make the choices that allow God's work in the world to be done. In other words, God offers us a partnership that will not only improve our lives but also the lives of others. However, we must be willing to make the choices that allow this partnership to flourish in our thoughts, words, and deeds. As powerful as God's love is, it relies on the choices we make to touch the lives of others.

After many years of thinking, I've come to feel strongly about these five parts of my belief in God and how God works in our lives to help us share our goodness with others. However, it took time for me to develop my thinking and my beliefs. Hopefully, the words and thoughts you find in this book will help expedite this process in your life.

God Is with Us—Today

The one thing I would add is that for me, believing in God does not require me to believe in events that took place a long time ago. Instead, I can feel that God is here with me *today*. I believe that confirming our belief in God is very much a current-day event. Further, because I can feel God's presence in my life, especially when I become aware of someone whom I care deeply about or who needs assistance in some way, it seems logical to me that God is with us now, helping us to become better people and leading us to help others however we can.

In summary, I believe:

- *God works through our hearts*: God guides our lives with love signals that we feel in our hearts. As such, most of us can confirm God's presence by paying closer attention to our feelings within, especially when they involve a need or problem that someone may have. In effect, God stirs us to action in this way.

- *God works through the lives we live*: God works in the world to help others by motivating us to respond to their needs. This is why it's so important to understand that we are not here just to help ourselves have a good life, but to help as many other people as possible to have good lives as well.

- *God works in the world around us*: I've experienced situations where God created circumstances that caused me to have certain experiences or to come into contact with certain people that either taught me something important or helped me accomplish something worthwhile. Clearly, God was at work around me in these instances, even though I was not aware of it at the time.

Regardless of what you believe at this moment, God is with you. As evidence, you have had feelings in your life that reflected your love or caring for someone close to you, or concern about someone in need whom you did not even know. You have already experienced God's presence in your life through these signals. In fact, God's presence is active in your life and mine, whether we raise our hands and ask for it or not. To allow that presence to change or even improve our lives, we have to pay attention to God's presence within and have the faith to make the choice to respond favorably to the directions God provides.

There are two freedoms:
the false one, where one is free to do what they like,
and the true one, where they are free to do what they ought.

CHARLES KINGSLEY

The Need for More Goodness in This World

There are thousands of religious groups and organizations in the world with varying views and beliefs about God. However, participation and membership in these groups are declining throughout the world while political differences, crimes, wars, and people in need are increasing.

It's time for everyone to start paying closer attention to God's love and goodness guidance at work within them. God is, in effect, *our goodness guide*. We just need more people to pay attention to God's guidance and follow it in their daily lives.

Wouldn't it be great . . .

- . . . if political and governmental leaders worldwide made the choice to work together under one simple belief: that each and every one of us, including them, has been put on this earth by God to help others have better lives?

- . . . if helping others became the guiding principle in every person's life, regardless of who they are or where they live?

- . . . if everyone became more concerned about the well-being and happiness of others, showing more concern for others than they show for themselves?

- . . . if we could replace the hate we have in our lives toward certain people with the love and goodness that God makes available to us?

- . . . if the people throughout the world would respond to the love provided by God and work together to make the world a safer and better place?

There's not much question that the world would be a better place if people everywhere worked to increase the amount of goodness coming from their lives. The need for more love and caring for each other is great. Unfortunately, hate is so abundant that it's going to take a real effort by millions of us to make love and goodness a priority.

God Has Equipped Us for This Work

We certainly don't come into the world as a finished product. There is a lot of development work required by parents, teachers, family, friends, and others, including ourselves, to get us to a productive point in our lives. A significant part of this development process, which frequently extends into our adult years, involves honing our ability to make good choices.

It's critical to look carefully within yourself to assess the interests, abilities, and feelings you've been given in order to determine what God is calling you to do. You have been given certain capabilities by God. The challenge for each of us is to identify these capabilities so that we can develop them further and fulfill the purpose to which God is calling us.

If there is one thing that will cement your belief in God, it is developing an understanding of the role that God wants and needs you to fulfill with your life. In so doing, you come to realize that you are an important member of God's team and that God has, in fact, equipped you for the role you have been called to fill.

No person has come to true greatness who has not felt
that, to some degree, their life belongs to others
and that what God gives them, God gives them for mankind.

PHILLIPS BROOKS

How About You?

As you read this book, I hope you will not only reflect on the words you find here, but also on your life and the roles that God, goodness, and helping others play in your day-to-day living. If you are focused primarily on yourself, there's no better time than now to accept a partnership with God and consider how you can make life better for other people.

Believing in God is not as complicated as some have made it. In effect, your choice to believe in God is a commitment to partner with God and use your life to help others whenever and wherever you can. This belief conveys a simple but fundamentally important principle—that using our lives to help others is the primary reason we were given a life and are here on earth today.

Signing up to partner with God is not a casual undertaking. It's the creation of life's most significant partnership: you and God working together to make the world a better place. Yes, this partnership will require a special effort on your part as you work to use your life to improve the lives of others. However, this focus on others will help you develop a way of living that will bring you a real sense of personal fulfillment and an honest feeling that you are making a difference with your life.

> *I slept and dreamt that life was joy.*
> *I awoke and saw that life was duty.*
> *I acted and behold, duty was joy.*

RABINDRANATH TAGORE

Example 2

A LOVE AND GOODNESS STORY

Boots for You, Boots for Me

Katherine went to a Chicago Bears game on a blustery winter day. She and her friends were bundled up for the occasion. But the wonderful thing that happened that day wasn't the Bears winning the game; it was Katherine's encounter with a homeless woman after the game. Katherine explained it this way.

I went to a Chicago Bears game. The high was only thirty degrees, so I layered up in a lot of clothing, including my new pair of winter boots.

After the game, we went to dinner. While we were inside, I became overheated, so I took off my heavy clothing and tossed it all into a bag.

We had a short walk to the train station. As we were walking across the street, I noticed a homeless woman crouched down trying to stay warm. The "walk" light appeared, and we hurried across the street to make sure we caught the train.

After I crossed the street, I felt something inside. For some reason, I was drawn to the woman I had just seen. I asked my friends to wait while I returned to talk with this woman.

As I approached, I noticed her cardboard sign that said, "I am in need of winter boots and winter clothes." Immediately, I knew this was providential timing and that I was supposed to give this woman the winter boots straight off my feet.

I asked her size and she said 8.5 (same as me). Everything I had in the bag was the right size for the woman: shirt, sweatshirt, gloves, and scarf.

The woman's boots were worn and wet. Mine were warm and waterproof. I handed her the bag of clothing I had taken off at dinner, along with my leftover pizza, and told her I would like to give her my boots.

The woman stood up and cried. I untied my boots, slid off my fuzzy warm socks, and handed them to her. She said they were the nicest shoes she'd ever had. We exchanged names and a few other words. We looked about the same age. We talked a lot—not through words as much as by looking at each other. When our eyes first met, the woman had looked worn and tired, but by the time I left, I could sense the warmth of her personality and the thankfulness in her heart.

I started to walk away when she said, "I don't want your feet to be cold. Can I give you my old boots?" She, who had nothing, offered me her boots. I wore them proudly all the way home. The woman's name was Amy, and I just cannot stop thinking about her.

If you have the urge to do something kind for someone, I encourage you to do it.

What a wonderful story. Not only did Katherine respond with love and goodness to the needs of the homeless woman, but she also had a feeling that divine guidance had put her in this spot. But Katherine didn't just feel sorry for the woman; she made the choice to actually do *something to help her. I have no doubt that God's love signal and Katherine's Spirit of Goodness were active in her life that day—and likely active in the homeless woman as well. Clearly, Katherine made a big difference in the woman's life, and I'm sure they will remember each other forever.*

CHAPTER 3

DEVELOPING YOUR SPIRIT OF GOODNESS

Opening Thought

E ach of us has a certain *life spirit* that conveys the kind of person we are to others. This spirit is comprised of many traits and qualities, including our honesty, kindness, intelligence, attitude, goals, and most of all, how we treat other people. If others feel better as a result of being around you, it's because you have developed a loving and caring life spirit that people can sense.

As part of this life spirit "package," God instills the beginnings of a *Spirit of Goodness* within us to help us focus on the needs of others and to motivate us to help others however we can. God leads us in a goodness direction, but our choices determine the degree to which we use our lives to help others. Our Spirit of Goodness can play a major role in the life we live if we continue to develop its influence in the choices we make each day.

What counts in life is not the mere fact that you have lived.
It is what difference you have made in the lives of others
that will determine the significance of the life you lead.

NELSON MANDELA

Spirits of Goodness

My Grandmother

My grandmother played a major teaching role in my life, not just with words but primarily through the way she lived her life and the example she set for me. She attended church every Sunday, walking the three blocks there and back regardless of the weather. She worked hard, five and a half days a week, as the seamstress in a local dress shop. And she cared deeply about people, not only phoning to check when someone was sick, but also mailing several birthday cards each week full of notes and personal "Granny words." When you received a card from Granny, you knew she cared about you.

The one verbal instruction she gave me that I remember to this day was, "Michael, if you can't say something nice about someone, don't say anything at all." I thank God for the love and caring that Granny showed me and how she cared about other people as well. I'm truly thankful for the example she provided, not just in what she believed, but also in how she lived and shared her love and goodness with others.

There was a definite spirit about Granny, and without question, it was her Spirit of Goodness. There was something about her and the way she cared about others that made her special. I was not the only one who considered her their Granny. Almost everyone in our small town called her Granny. They felt a special attachment to her because of the way she showed that she truly cared about them.

My Friend Ed

My friend Ed was one super guy. He was always positive, always interested in what you had to say, and always greeted you with a big smile. Ed had an upbeat spirit that you could sense when you were with him. He possessed that wonderful ability to make everyone who knew him feel like they were his best friend. Every time I was with Ed, I just felt better.

Unfortunately, cancer took Ed's life many years ago. Nevertheless, seldom does a week go by that I don't think about him and wish he were back here lifting our spirits again. Ed gave us something special—a good feeling about ourselves—and I value his friendship to this day. Ed cared about people, and all his friends experienced his Spirit of Goodness when they were with him.

Those Post-Hurricane Volunteers

While I was writing this book, the country experienced one of its worst and largest hurricanes—Hurricane Helene, which worked its way from the Gulf Coast up through North Carolina, destroying thousands of homes and businesses, and in some cases wiping out entire small towns. Watching a televised report one week later, I was impressed by the hundreds of volunteers who drove to North Carolina to help in any way they could.

One female homeowner reported, "This gentleman showed up at my house with his chainsaw in hand and simply asked, 'What can I do to help you?'" Another young woman whose recently opened art store was filled with mud said, "I looked up from my tears and there were several men with shovels who then spent two days cleaning out my shop so that I could start to rebuild." No question, there are many Spirits of Goodness at work in this world.

Where did my grandmother, my friend Ed, and these post-hurricane volunteers get the Spirit of Goodness that guided their lives and their concern for others?

- *God gave them a basic Spirit of Goodness*: I believe that God gives each of us an initial Spirit of Goodness so that we are pre-equipped to help God improve the lives of others. I believe this because God puts us here to help others have better lives, and we need the motivation of our Spirit of Goodness to help us do that.

- *They took the spirit that God gave them and further developed it*: How our God-given Spirit of Goodness develops within our lives depends on us and on the choices we make. God gives us a good start, but it is left to us to make something special out of the Spirit of Goodness that we're given. Parents, teachers, and friends may help us along the way, but ultimately, you and I determine the role that our Spirit of Goodness will play in our lives.

God wants us to use our lives to help others and to work to make the world a better place. God indicates this through the love signals that God sends to our hearts. It is our Spirit of Goodness that helps us respond to God and motivates us to make the choices needed to turn God's signals into the *love*, *help*, and *hope* that so many people need.

You Can Override Your Spirit of Goodness

Many of us override our Spirit of Goodness by focusing on ourselves and not being that concerned about others. This, of course, is a selfish way to live and seldom, if ever, brings true happiness to anyone. The good news, however, is that you can change such an inward focus if you make the choice to do so.

I recommend that you focus on the goodness coming from your life and on the development of the Spirit of Goodness God has given you. Yes, God instills a basic Spirit of Goodness within us and activates it to a greater degree if we ask God to do so. But it's still up to us and the choices we make to develop our Spirit of Goodness more fully in our lives.

There is nothing we can do to improve our life experience and bring us satisfaction like spreading goodness does. The world and the people in it need our goodness. In addition, we need to share our goodness with others as part of our work to develop meaningful and worthwhile lives.

Here are three things to keep in mind as you consider the role goodness plays in your life:

- *Our basic purpose in life is to help others:* You and I are here not solely to develop our own lives, but equally important, to help others develop their lives as well. Sharing our goodness with people not only helps to improve their lives but our lives too. It is an often overlooked fact that we help ourselves by helping others.

- *God welcomes our help:* God needs our help to make the world a better place. There are millions of people in this world right now who have issues, problems, and needs that our goodness could greatly help. You and I and millions of others need to *do* more to make other people's lives better.

- *Sharing goodness is a fundamentally important ingredient in a meaningful life:* Responding to God's love signals with our goodness is key to making our lives exceptional. Our lives work much better and we achieve so much more when we consider our daily living as a partnership with God to spread more goodness in this world.

It's important to recognize that sharing your goodness with others is a *basic* or *foundational* requirement in achieving meaning and happiness in your life. When you share your goodness and help others, you not only make them feel better, but you also feel better about yourself and the way you're living your life.

Telling a gossipy tale about someone or making a sarcastic remark in someone's absence might provide you with a momentary high, but these types of comments or actions don't improve your life or the lives of others in any way. Instead of falling prey to such derogatory words or actions—and many more that are worse—you should focus on increasing the *good words* and *helpful actions* coming from your life. That's how you make your life special, meaningful, and worthwhile.

Developing Your Spirit of Goodness

When you commit to developing your Spirit of Goodness, you are signing up to turn God's love into words, deeds, and actions that help someone in some way. It may be a personal problem that you help someone resolve. You might volunteer with a nonprofit organization, or visit the neighbor down the street who lives alone, or help teach a class at church or school. You could also work to help people in special ways through your career, vocation, or life role.

One mental activity that will help you develop your Spirit of Goodness is to reflect each morning on how you might be kind today or use your life to help someone in a special way. Yes, you have plenty to worry about, but why not start your day thinking about what you might do to make someone's life a little better? Then, check back with yourself in the evening to reflect on the goodness you shared that helped or benefitted another person in some way.

No man or woman can really be strong, gentle, and good
without the world being better for it,
without somebody being helped and comforted
by the very existence of that goodness.

PHILLIPS BROOKS

Like many things in life, the development of our Spirit of Goodness requires practice. This will require a conscious effort initially, but as you take note of the reactions of those you are able to help, it will become routine for you. Not only will you be a better person as a result, but others' lives will be better as well.

God's Love Signals and Our Spirit of Goodness

In summary, I believe God's *love* and our *goodness* work in our lives this way:

- *God guides us through love signals in our hearts:* As I believe it to be, God touches and guides our lives through the love and caring we feel for someone or some circumstance. The love signals provided to us by God awaken something inside us, create special feelings within us, and help us identify good and positive things that we can and should do with our lives.

- *Our Spirit of Goodness helps us respond to God's love signals:* In addition to the guiding love that God provides, our Spirit of Goodness can further motivate us to actually *say* or *do* something in response to God's love touching our life in some way. In other words, God awakens us to special needs, and our Spirit of Goodness helps us turn God's love signals into words and actions that help someone in some way.

> *Do all the good you can, in all ways you can,*
> *to all the people you can, in every place you can,*
> *at all times you can, with all the zeal you can,*
> *for as long as you can.*
>
> JOHN WESLEY

My Personal Experience

I can feel God's love signaling me when I become aware of someone in need. Not long after, I become aware of my Spirit of Goodness working in my head about the circumstances and helping me think through what I should say or do as a result. God's love touches my heart, and my Spirit of Goodness helps me think things through and determine more specifically what I should do.

I've witnessed people responding to these same influences as they made choices that helped someone and showed that they truly cared about them. I've seen people pull over and give an unhoused person money so they could get something to eat. I've seen individuals travel to another country to help build a new medical clinic for the people there. I've seen a family member buy a small house trailer for a sister so she and her two children would have a decent place to live. I've seen a neighbor make trips to the grocery store for a friend who was confined to their bed at home.

These examples, and millions like them, are proof to me that God and many Spirits of Goodness are alive in the world and working to motivate us to use our lives to help others in many different ways.

God, You, and Others

As you do your belief-development work about God and how God might help you live a better life, reflect on how God can guide you to use your life to help others. I now understand that God helps us not just to be believers but also to be doers, and to help others have better and more meaningful lives. That's why God instilled the beginnings of a Spirit of Goodness in each of us and why we need to work diligently to develop that spirit within us.

Active Spirits of Goodness: A Worldwide Need

With all the conflicts and turmoil taking place in the world, there is no question about the need for more active Spirits of Goodness in the lives of people everywhere. Yes, there are millions of good people and a lot of goodness being shared throughout the world today. However, we need millions more—citizens and leaders alike—to recognize the need for more goodness and to join a worldwide effort to share our goodness with one another.

With the publication of *Love and Goodness*, I'm urging people everywhere to respond to God's love signals as well as to the thoughtful nudging of their Spirits of Goodness. I'm challenging all who read this book to become part of a goodness revolution by letting God and their Spirit of Goodness be active influences in their lives. Sharing our goodness—each of us doing our part to help others—is the way we improve our lives while making the world a better place.

Protecting Your Spirit of Goodness

Our life development work is heavily influenced these days by outside sources, including information on the internet, friends offering unsound advice, and supposedly responsible individuals such as politicians, athletes, and entertainers. Be careful who you listen to and work hard not to have your understanding and insights concerning your life's Spirit of Goodness sidetracked by an unreliable source.

Deceivers are the most dangerous members of society.
They trifle with the best affections of our nature
and violate the most sacred obligations.

GEORGE CRABBE

A reality of life is that we are prone to making selfish choices, to doing what feels good in the moment. Sometimes, in response to pressure from so-called friends, we make a poor choice instead of doing the right or more important thing. We have the power to make choices that block or negate the influence of God's love signals and the work of our Spirits of Goodness. When we make bad choices, we not only miss opportunities to help others, but we also miss opportunities to make important contributions to the positive development of our own lives.

Instead, you have to feel and interpret what's going on inside you. Take note of the love signals God is sending you. Listen to your Spirit of Goodness working to help you make good and effective choices. No question, God and your Spirit of Goodness will provide you with needed life development support if you are willing to pay attention and respond in a positive way to the guidance and motivation they provide.

Example 3

A LOVE AND GOODNESS STORY

Safety and Goodness

This example illustrates that our lives need to be oriented toward love and goodness for us to recognize the opportunities to make a real difference in someone's life. We can help people in special ways if we pay attention to God's love at work within us and then follow our Spirit of Goodness by actually doing *something that helps someone in a special way. Officer Fred Williams did exactly that.*

While responding to the call of a child riding in a vehicle not secured in a car seat, Officer Fred Williams met a young mom and her three-year-old daughter.

"When I spoke to her, she was very forthcoming and knew that the child should be in a booster seat," Officer Williams explained. "She admitted that she was wrong and that she had recently fallen on hard times."

Instead of ticketing her, Officer Williams told her to meet him at a nearby Walmart so he could buy a booster seat for her daughter. "It was the easiest money I ever spent," he said. "It's something that anybody could do, especially when a child's safety is involved."

The young mother said the generous officer's selfless act gave her some much-needed hope. "He could have just given me a ticket and gotten me in a whole lot of trouble, but instead, out of the goodness of his heart and out of his own pocket, he did something for me and my family that I'll never forget," she said. "He went above and beyond to protect a little girl and helped a family that can't help themselves right now."

Nothing will ever give you so much personal satisfaction as when someone sincerely thanks you for something special you did for them, especially when it was unexpected. So, when you encounter someone in need, make the choice to do *something, as Officer Williams did.*

CHAPTER 4

CONFIRMING YOUR BELIEFS

Opening Thought

One of the realities of life is that we, as individuals, develop over time. Our knowledge, wisdom, abilities, physical bodies, and communication skills develop and usually improve as we grow. In addition, as we get older, our belief in God typically comes into sharper focus, and we tend to think more carefully about the presence of God in the world and in our lives.

Supporting this personal growth are experiences—good ones and some bad ones—that create challenging times in our lives. Such experiences help us gain insights into how to manage our lives more effectively. In addition, they help us understand our need for God's guidance in our lives.

Recognizing the potential benefit of having God's love and direction in your life is a starting point. It then takes some time, some careful thinking, some prayerful conversations with God, and even some trial runs in which you respond to God's love signals by doing what you believe God is leading you to do. Somewhere during this process, most of us will realize that we need and want God to be an active partner in our lives.

*Life's greatest achievement is
the continual remaking of yourself
so that at last you know how to live.*

WINIFRED RHODES

Should Believing Be as Complicated as We Have Made It?

According to Gallup, the number of people who attend organized religious activities regularly is declining, and is now just over 30 percent of the US population. Further, there is an increasing number who are not members of any church, now just over 50 percent of us in the US. When you consider that at the same time *over 80 percent of our population reports that they believe in God,* this lack of participation in organized religious activities is surprising.

Why is this? One of the factors contributing to these circumstances is that many organized religions have made believing in God difficult to understand, frequently requiring the potential believer to accept some sensational events that happened a long time ago as part of the belief package. In other words, we have made believing in God more of a history lesson than an understanding that God is here with us *today,* helping us say kind words and do good things for others.

I believe that God is our most important spiritual influence and has a loving interest in each of us as well as the ability to guide our lives in good and positive ways. If there are two words that characterize God's influence in our lives, they must be *love* and *goodness* because it's God's *daily love* and our *daily goodness* that help us develop and live meaningful and effective lives.

Far be it from me to explain God in a simple way or convey a "this is the way it is" message. However, I can tell you what I believe—and feel—about the presence of God in my life in the hope that it will help you confirm your beliefs as well. As I see it, believing in God—and feeling God's presence within us—is not as complicated as many, unintentionally or otherwise, have made it to be.

Feeling God's Presence in Our Lives

Millions of us have confirmed that we have felt God's presence in our lives. That presence is a special feeling that enters through our hearts and motivates us to do good and helpful things not only for ourselves, but for others as well. There are three types of experiences I have had that reconfirm my belief in God:

- *I have felt God's signals motivate me to do good and helpful things for others:* As stated many times in this book, I believe God speaks to us through our hearts. God sends us love signals that direct us to be kind to people or to help someone in some special way. Simply stated, we're here to help God take care of the people on this earth. To accomplish this, God directs us through the love and concerns we feel in our hearts to care for others and to help people however we can.

- *My life works better when I follow God's signals:* Whenever I respond positively to God's influence by being kind to someone, by helping someone in need, or by doing something God is directing me to do (such as writing this book), I can tell that my life is working better, and I in fact feel better about myself. For me, these "feel better" moments are God confirming to me that I have done the right thing in making the choice to follow where God was leading me to go.

- *I've seen God work in the world by leading people to devote their lives to helping others through the careers, vocations, or roles that God has called them to fill:* Another point that confirms my belief in God is that God also leads us to use our lives to help others in committed and long-term ways. Many of us live ineffective lives because we have chosen to do "our thing" instead of the thing God has called us to do. God can improve, even change, our lives if we take note of the signals God provides and work to follow the life path that God has designed for us.

I share these personal beliefs and feelings about God in the hope that they will help you develop your beliefs as well. However, this chapter is about you and your efforts to affirm what you believe. So, let's get back to a few suggestions concerning how you might do that.

Approaches to Confirming Your Beliefs

There are three approaches you can take to confirm your religious beliefs and live according to them:

- *Become a practicing member of a church or religious group*: You can become a practicing member of an organized religious group or church (or reconfirm an existing membership within one of the many religions in the world) and accept their views and understandings about God's role in your life.

- *Be independent and chart your own course*: You can decide not to be affiliated with any organized church or group and instead form your own views about God.

- *Combine the two*: You can become an active member of an organized church or group (or reconfirm an existing membership) while also working out what you believe about God, and more importantly, how those beliefs will help you live a better life.

I recommend the third alternative. Let me tell you why.

I believe God's love is with us no matter what we have done or how we have lived up to now. While religious organizations can help us in many ways, it's not these churches or groups that open the door to God. No, God has already opened that door and is with us right now, no matter what. There is nothing special we had to do for God's love signals to become a part of our lives and become available to help us live in better and more helpful ways, *except for two things*:

- First, we have to confirm our acceptance of our partnership with God by turning to God in prayer and asking God to help us live a good and effective life.
- Second, we have to start making good and respectful choices that allow us to help others and carry out God's work in the world through the lives we live.

You don't have to attend a church or special group to find God and experience God's presence in your life. But you do need the involvement with the church's or group's members—and with other people through their work and outreach programs—to prove to yourself that living under God's guidance of helping others is how you want to live your life.

You might be able to confirm your beliefs on your own. You can find lots of ways to help others in your neighborhood or city if you look for them. However, most established churches and religious groups provide proven and active opportunities to get involved in one or more of their outreach programs and to talk and work with people who are on their belief journey as well.

This is the high function of the church.
It calls its members to enter into social and civic movements.
It seeks to fill its members with such moral courage
and spiritual power that they become
part of the world's solution.

RALPH W. SOCKMAN

God Works Primarily Through People

As you formulate or reconfirm your beliefs, it's important to note that most of God's work in the world is accomplished through people.

Therefore, belonging to an organized religious group provides you with more opportunities to think about what you actually believe while also giving you more opportunities to be of service to God by helping fellow members and others in your community or around the world.

Well-organized churches and religious groups typically have many ongoing programs and projects to help others in some way—far more than you would likely ever come up with on your own. Practicing your religious beliefs by helping others is what life is all about. Such actions help you to be or become a conduit for God's work here on earth.

Here is an excellent example of how God works through people:

> *When discussing how God works through people to help others, I have asked people to consider this question: Did God build St. Jude Children's Research Hospital in Memphis, Tennessee, where thousands of young people have been cured of childhood cancer at no expense to their parents or family? My answer to this question is yes, God definitely did. But God didn't do it by sending bricks and mortar down from Heaven. God did it through Danny Thomas, who made the choice to do something special in support of St. Jude, and through the thousands of medical professionals and millions of donors who have supported this work.*

In my opinion, the key to living a successful life is to listen to how God and your Spirit of Goodness are calling you to help others and to make choices that allow you to make life better for others in some way. This is the most important partnership you will ever have. You are dependent on God's love and direction and the motivation of your Spirit of Goodness, and they are dependent on you to make the choices that allow this partnership to achieve great and important things for others here on earth.

All is not evil in America, nor is the country hopeless.
The forces that make for good are greater than the forces
that make for evil,
but they must have human channels through which
they can flow.

GORDON H. BAKER

Working at Believing

You have to think *and* work to identify and confirm what you feel inside, and correspondingly, what you believe. I've been thinking about some of the points in this book for over fifty years, but I'm sure you can complete such an evaluation in less time than that. Believing in God and understanding that your Spirit of Goodness is at work in your life are critical, but it takes some real effort on our part to confirm the feelings that support those beliefs.

You can start your "believing work" by simply being nicer to people. Smiles, handshakes, and sincere inquiries concerning someone's well-being are good places to start. You can select a church or religious group to join, or become more active where you are already a member and have greater contact with others who are working on their beliefs as well. You can look for specific opportunities to help someone in your community or to participate in a local nonprofit organization.

As you become more active in these and other helpful ways, I would encourage you to talk to God via prayers—short ones, long ones, even simple conversations with God during your day—not only to relate the experiences you are having in developing your beliefs, but also to ask for God's guidance as you work through your build-my-beliefs experiences.

As you do this belief development work, take special note of the feelings within you when you see or hear about someone in need. Support those feelings with some choices to help others in some way. You only have to touch a few lives in small but helpful ways to confirm that you are here to do God's work and that managing your life in concert with *love* and *goodness* is the way to do it.

> *God deals with us whether in sickness or in health,*
> *whether in prosperity or adversity,*
> *whether in good or in evil days,*
> *whether in life or in death,*
> *not according to our merit, but*
> *according to God's mercy and love.*

ALBERT J. PENNER

Example 4

A LOVE AND GOODNESS STORY

Mulie's Love and Goodness

What's a story about a cat doing in a book like this? Well, I learned something important about love and goodness recently, something that I had not really thought about or written about in the past. If you'll allow me a bit of personal privilege, I'd like to tell you about a special cat named Mulie.

Mulie, a friendly cat who wandered up our back steps over fifteen years ago and has lived with us ever since, died today. He was getting along in years, so it was not a total surprise that he passed away. What was a surprise to me was that I suddenly felt so sad that he was gone. I didn't think I would feel this way, but I'm really down that he is no longer here with us.

My wife and I buried him in our backyard this morning. As I was covering him with the dirt we'd dug up to prepare his grave, I couldn't help but cry. The reality of Mulie no longer being with us was sinking in and taking a toll on me. But after thinking about Mulie's life and the overall circumstances, something became clear to me. Mulie taught me something important about love and goodness, and I want to share it with you.

Before I do, let me offer a few unique details about Mulie:

- He was not a handsome cat. Instead of naming him Ugly, we settled for Mulie.

- He had a terrible moaning meow that sometimes woke us up at night.

- He shed on our living room sofa, requiring frequent cleanups.
- He would paw the water out of his water bowl, requiring cleanup every morning.
- He refused to use the cat box, instead requiring strategically placed dog pads.
- He would occasionally make a mistake and do a "number two" under our bed.

Naturally, you're wondering why in the world I'm sad if I won't have to clean up after a cat like Mulie anymore. Well, let me summarize why.

I won't have those loving moments when Mulie would join me in my favorite chair, lie down right next to my leg, and purr. I won't have those bedtime experiences when Mulie would jump up on the bed, climb on my chest, and bump my chin with his head to show his affection. I won't have those special winter times in front of the fireplace when Mulie would trot back and forth between my wife's chair and mine, ever the politician, showing that he cared for us both. And I won't have those passing moments during the day when Mulie and I exchanged greetings, even though he was deaf and couldn't hear a word I was saying.

I could go on, but you can see Mulie was a major source of affection—of love and goodness—in my life. So, what did Mulie and his life teach me? Simply this: In spite of all his unique "habits" that required special cleanups, his love and goodness were his most important qualities. As I thought about the circumstances, it became clear that I was missing Mulie's love and goodness, and that was what made him such a special fellow to us.

So it is with you and me. It doesn't matter . . .

- what we look like.
- how we dress.

- how we express our love for someone.
- how unique we are.
- that we have unusual habits.

What matters is . . .

- our willingness to share our love and goodness with others.
- how we make others feel as a result of our interactions with them.
- that we use our lives to make others' lives a little better and more enjoyable.

Thank you, Mulie, for teaching me this crucial lesson—that love and goodness are far more important than the many "things" we place so much value on. I'll forever be grateful for the love and goodness you shared with us while you were here.

As you focus on areas in your life that you want to improve, don't waste too much time on "things" like clothes, tattoos, hairstyles, phones, or the car you drive. Instead, take stock of the amount of love and goodness coming from your life and how much your love and goodness are likely to be missed when you are no longer here.

CHAPTER 5

DOES IT REALLY MATTER
WHAT YOU BELIEVE?

Opening Thought

Does it really matter what you believe?
This is an important question, one that people can help you with but that you ultimately have to answer for yourself. To do so, you have to take some time to live according to your beliefs to verify that they help you create and live a more meaningful and effective life. In other words, believing in God is one part, but how those beliefs improve your daily living is the other.

Get the pattern of your life from God.
Then, go about your work and be yourself.

PHILLIPS BROOKS

Maybe It Doesn't Matter What You Believe

Maybe there's no Heaven or Hell. Maybe there's no afterlife for you to be concerned about. Maybe it doesn't actually matter what you believe. Just live your life however you like, make the most money

49

you can, and have as much fun as possible. Maybe that's the way you should do it.

After all, we see more and more people living in less than godly ways. And with thousands of religions in the world and millions of non-believers as well, when it comes to believing in God, there is no worldwide consensus as to what is right or wrong.

Many of us simply don't want to be bothered by God. We'd rather be free to do or say whatever we like. We like to impress others, sometimes with questionable words and actions. However, many times, such words and actions turn out to be poor choices. When reality sinks in, we often come to regret what we said or how we conducted ourselves. At the time, it seemed cute or pleasurable, but this so-called fun-only, do-whatever-feels-good lifestyle almost always works out to be a disappointment.

It doesn't matter what *others* believe; what matters is what *you* believe—and, as a result of those beliefs, how you live *your* life. Believing in God is a personal decision. Yes, it helps if you have family and friends who influence you in positive ways as they share their love and goodness with you. Participating in faith-based groups and events can also provide you with helpful experiences. But in the end, the decision to believe in God and let that belief guide your life is a personal one. It's yours and yours alone to make.

> *There is no better measure of a person*
> *than what they do when they are*
> *absolutely free to choose.*

WILMA ASKINAS

Assessing the Need for God in Your Life

Many people simply don't bother to make a personal assessment of their faith in God. By avoiding such an exercise, they give themselves permission to skip what is clearly one of the most important evaluations anyone can ever make. I say that because recognizing God's influence in our lives can help us, more than anything, to live in a meaningful and productive way.

As you think about establishing—or reconfirming—your relationship with God, consider these four questions:

- *Could you and your life benefit from an influence that motivates, and on occasion even pushes, you to help others in some way?* One of the most important factors in living a meaningful life is to help others have better lives as well. God's love signals and our God-blessed Spirit of Goodness can help us do exactly that.

- *Could you and your life benefit from having a special guide to help you through tough times or work through important projects?* I can't tell you how many times I've turned to God in prayer while writing this book, asking for assistance to help me determine not only what to say about a specific point, but how to say it as well. In fact, I should have listed God as the co-author of this book.

- *Could you and your life benefit from sincere guidance in determining how your interests, abilities, and feelings are leading you to the purpose of your life?* Since God gave you these qualities, there is no one better than God to help you determine the work, role, or vocation these qualities are calling you to pursue.

- *Could you and your life benefit from having someone who is always with you to share their love and motivate your goodness as you go about your life each day?* By allowing God to be active in our lives, we create a partnership that will help us not only to be better people, but also to accomplish more with our lives.

Take your time to think through your answers to these four questions and the areas of life they address. You may even write your answers down and edit them until you feel you have developed answers that are right for you. At that point, you'll be in a good position to determine for yourself the degree to which you want to have—and need—God to be an active participant in your life.

Keep These Two Points in Mind

Here are two additional points that have helped me and that I have come to strongly believe. They may help you as well as you review and think about your belief in God:

- *God works in the world through the goodness of people*: God is active ("at work") in our lives through the love we feel in our hearts and, subsequently, the goodness we share with others. God's love is the spiritual thread that, in effect, connects people in this world together. It is our belief in God (the source of all love) and responding to our Spirit of Goodness (the motivation that helps us turn that love into helpful words and actions) that conditions and guides us to live in effective ways. If everyone's belief in God were strong enough, the world would be a very peaceful, happy, and helpful place.

- *God needs us to help*: God needs you, me, and millions of others to pay attention to the love signals we feel inside and to respond to the influence of our Spirit of Goodness to help carry out God's work in the world. Partnering with God to help others is without question the most important project you and I could ever have.

I've had some pushback from a few people about my point of God needing us to help. They stressed to me that God can "do anything" and is not dependent on us. However, I don't believe God works that way but instead works primarily through people like you and me.

While I do believe that God sends love signals to us, in most instances they're leading us to say or do something that helps improve another person's life in some way. Therefore, God needs millions of boots on the ground working to make the world better for everyone.

God needs *all of us* to become partners in the work to make life better for people everywhere.

If you believe in spreading love and goodness, you believe in God's work. If you believe in helping others have better and more enjoyable lives, you believe in God's work. If you've noted how much better you feel when you've said something nice or done something helpful for someone, you've proven the positive effect of making God's love and your goodness priorities in your life.

So, Maybe It Does Matter

As you ponder the role that God and your Spirit of Goodness play, or might play, in your life, there are several things you should consider. Believing in God and that God is always with you will have several positive effects on you and your life:

- *Your life will have direction and meaning*: As I have stated several times in this book, I believe that God and our Spirit of Goodness have been with us from the very beginning of our lives. If we pay attention, we can feel their helpful presence directing our lives. Those who believe in God have an almost endless number of opportunities to confirm that presence by noting the tugs on their heart that motivate them to be respectful of others and to respond to the needs of people in various ways. Believing in God provides direction and meaning to our lives when we understand and accept that we are here to help God help others in some way.

- *You will be a better person*: You will be a better person as you respond to the love that God awakens in your life and to the guidance that your Spirit of Goodness provides. You will not be going it alone; instead, you will have these two critical influences helping you live a good and effective life.

- *You will help more people*: You will help more people and make life better for others as you live under the love of God and the guidance of your Spirit of Goodness. You will be able to utilize your interests, abilities, and feelings (your purpose) in more effective ways.

- *You will be an example for others to follow*: More people will respect you if you live your life in this positive, helpful, God-inspired way. Your life will inspire family, friends, and others to make a positive difference in this world and in the lives of other people.

Believing in God and that God works in your life through the love in your heart will provide your life with a foundation upon which you can build a more worthwhile life. The objective of living to help others, as God is motivating us to do, is basically what you sign up for when you confirm your belief in God to yourself, to others, and to God. You may not understand every last detail about God, but you can quickly grasp that living your life to improve the lives of others, even in small ways, will improve your life as well.

Your Beliefs Matter, but Don't Forget Your Works

Some organized religions support the notion that believing is the primary thing and that works are secondary or not required to validate our beliefs. That premise just never felt right to me. It seems perfectly logical that my belief in God should be reflected in my words and deeds, and significantly so. Further, a major part of my belief is that God has called me to use my talents and my life to help others in some way. Therefore, I believe our words and actions (our "works") are evidence of whether we actually believe in God or just say we do.

Keep this point in mind: God works in the world primarily through people. As examples, God delivers the meal to the elderly couple down the street through the goodness of the neighbor who prepares it and takes it to them. God provides opportunities for young people to learn through the teacher who has dedicated her life to childhood development. God provides important corrective surgery through the physician and trained professionals who have dedicated their lives to helping and healing the sick. It's easy for me to see that God works through people. Therefore, our works are almost as important as our beliefs.

Whatever your vocation or life role might be—one of thousands of possibilities you might be led to pursue and fulfill—it can be executed in more worthwhile ways if you believe that the basic reason you are here is to carry out God's work in the world, and in so doing, to share your goodness with others.

To have integrity, individuals
cannot merely be weather vanes turning briskly
with every doctrinal wind that blows.
They must possess key loyalties and key convictions
which can serve as a basis of judgment
and a standard of action.

JOHN STUDEBAKER

It's a Choice You Make

You see or read about people every day who have done positive things and helped others in some way. They are examples of how good choices improve someone's life. On the other hand, you read about people who have committed crimes or hurt others in some way. They are examples of how poor choices damage the quality of your life. How you elect to live your life—in good or bad ways—is a choice. And believing in God is another important choice that is left to you to make.

Believing in God or reconfirming a belief that you developed long ago is a choice you can make at any time—even right now if you feel so led.

- You don't have to join an established religious group or organization to start practicing your belief in God.

- You don't have to complete any special training or an indoctrination program so that you will "think right" about things.
- You don't have to be approved by a special membership committee.

Instead, you just have to accept the presence of God's love in your life, advise God of your acceptance, and start sharing that love and your goodness with others as you live your life each day.

Be Sure to Touch Base with God

If you make the life-improving choice to welcome God into your life or to reconfirm a similar choice you made some time ago, communicate your choice to God via a prayer in which you ask for God's guidance. Ask God to help you to help others through the interests, abilities, and feelings that God has given you, the love that God awakens within you from time to time, and the influence of your Spirit of Goodness that motivates you to say or do something helpful when you see a need for it.

With this choice, you commit to making a difference in the lives of others by sharing the love and goodness that God has inspired within you. May God bless you in a special way as you work to use your love and goodness to improve the lives of others.

> *Faith is kept alive in us and gathers strength*
> *more from practice than speculation.*
>
> JOSEPH ADDISON

If You Need To, Keep Working at It

I don't want to provide an escape hatch right here in the middle of the book. Therefore, if you want or need to make this decision, I urge you to confirm your belief in God now to yourself and, through a prayer, to God as well. However, for those who are reluctant to make a firm choice to believe in God right now, you can start an "under further evaluation" process by doing these two things:

- *Check how you feel when you become aware of someone in need*: The next time someone with a special need (you may or may not know them personally) comes to your attention, take note of how you feel about them and their situation. Odds are, you will feel God speaking to you through your heart about this person, their circumstances, and their needs. This communication with God comes naturally when you become aware of someone who needs help with life in some way.

- *Reach out and help someone*: When you become aware of an individual you could help in some way, do it. Reach out and do whatever you can to help them improve their situation. When you do, take note of how your Spirit of Goodness nudged you to say or do something to improve, even in a small way, another person's life. And take note of how following God's lead to live with goodness makes you feel.

I urge you to do these two things to take stock of how believing in God and living this way might improve your life. Remember, although it helps, you don't have to be an active member of a church, synagogue, or special group to follow where God is leading you to go. You just need to make the choice to follow God's love signals and start doing things that make life better for yourself and for others.

Faith is to believe what we do not see,
and the reward of this faith is to see what we believe.

ST. AUGUSTINE

Example 5

A LOVE AND GOODNESS STORY

Learning About Goodness at an Early Age

Love and goodness are not adult-only activities, and this class of fifth graders proved it when they joined together to help one of their classmates in a special way. There are a lot of things one can learn in school, but making the choice to help another person has to be the most important. If you have young children, this is a great love and goodness story to share with them.

After a group of students in a small town in Texas learned that their fellow student, Jason, was colorblind, they pooled their allowance money to buy him special glasses. They bought two pairs of EnChroma glasses, one for inside and one for outside. The glasses allowed Jason to distinguish colors for the first time in his life.

The students collected the money in secret and then surprised Jason with the glasses at school one day. Jason's parents were there for the moment and were blown away by the children's kind gesture.

"Witnessing the outpouring of compassion toward Jason and the unharnessed joy in the faces of so many children was a moment I will never forget," his mother said.

Jason will have to relearn the names of colors and shades, but a couple of his classmates have already stepped forward to volunteer their help by making flashcards and coaching him. For Jason, the gift is more than just a way for him to be able to see the world more vividly; it's confirmation that his peers care about him.

"I'm just really excited because I know that my friends are really true friends for doing this for me," he said. "I can't believe this is happening!"

We are never too young (or too old) to learn the benefits of living in this helpful way. No question, Jason was deeply touched and grateful for what his fellow classmates did. And these students experienced a wonderful feeling as a result of the special present they provided.

I think every school class in the United States should complete at least one love and goodness project each year (a project each quarter would be even better). Helping students develop an understanding of love and goodness seems to be as important as reading, writing, and arithmetic—maybe even more so.

A ROAD TEST FOR LIVING
A HELPFUL LIFE

Opening Thought

Most of us have heard the phrase, "Try it; you'll like it." It's a bit of a challenge, often used in a sales situation to help the seller prove to the potential buyer that the product or service works as advertised.

Although I'm not trying to sell you anything, I would encourage you to try living a helpful life for several months, making choices that assist others and that make their lives a little better in some way. See how conducting yourself this way makes you feel. If it makes you feel better about your life and yourself, I hope you'll sign a long-term contract for living this way.

Your life mirrors what you put into it or withhold from it.
When you are lazy, it is lazy.
When you hold back, it holds back.
When you hesitate, it stands there staring, hands in pockets.
But when you commit, it comes on like blazes.

GREGG LEVOY

Three Important Points About Life

We're so busy with our daily routines—including school, work, and family activities—that we seldom stop to think about what we need to manage our lives effectively. We tend to live our lives one day at a time without an overall strategy for how best to do so. If we aren't careful, we can live our entire lives without ever understanding how our choices define who we are and what we ultimately achieve.

Our goals are important. But it's the choices we make in support of our goals that determine if we achieve them or not. With good choices and the willingness to see them through, we can accomplish almost anything. Our choices not only determine if we will achieve our goals, but they also determine the type of person we become.

I'd like to outline three important points about life and the basic choices associated with them:

- *We are here for each other:* You and I are not here to live our lives just for ourselves, but to help others have better lives as well. If there is a secret to living a meaningful and fulfilling life, it's focusing on the needs of others. Using your life to help others is what it's all about. *You can make the choice to devote much of your life to helping people in your own special way,* or *you can make the choice to be generally unconcerned about those around you.*

- *Our life has a built-in purpose:* If we are attentive to our interests, our abilities, and the feelings we have about the needs of others, our purpose will at some point become clear to us. You and I are here for a reason: to do something special with our lives. It's up to each of us to determine what that is. *You can make the choice to work to discover what you were brought into this world to do,* or *you can make the choice to ignore the true purpose of your life.*

- *There is some goodness in everyone:* No matter our past, we still have an opportunity to increase the goodness our life produces through the future choices we make. It may include showing concern for friends and neighbors, reaching out to improve your community, or devoting your life to a work or cause that would make the world a better place. *You can make the choice to increase the good deeds you do,* or *you can make the choice to ignore the need to expand the goodness you share with others and with the world.*

Take a moment to think about how powerful your choices really are. You can use them to accomplish good, meaningful, and even great things with your life, or your choices can create difficulties, hurt people, and be the reason you miss the opportunity to do something special with the life you have been given. No question, our choices define who we are today and who we will become in the future.

Where Do You Fit on the Lifestyle Scale?

While there are many lifestyles that may match the way we live our lives, we might consider the two extremes of the lifestyle scale for self-evaluation purposes:

- *Selfish and self-centered*: On one end is what I would call a selfish, self-centered lifestyle. We all know people like this: individuals who talk and act as though life is all about them and who care little or nothing about other people's happiness and well-being.

- *Helpful and kind-hearted*: On the other end of this scale are the helpful, kind-hearted folks who always seem to be concerned about others and willing to help in any way they can. Almost without exception, we enjoy being around people like this.

Most of us live somewhere in between these two extremes. However, as you make the choices that manage your life and living, the closer you get to *the helpful end* of things, the happier you will be and the more meaningful your life will be to others.

Help thy brother's boat across,
and lo, thine own has reached the shore.

HINDU PROVERB

More than Just Believing

As I've mentioned several times in this book, I don't believe that "just believing" is enough. Our belief in God should not remain a mental or internal exercise but should influence, and heavily so, what we say and do each day. Specifically, it should guide and influence us to help God care for the people on this earth. It's not just the feelings you develop in church on Sunday. It's also what you say and do the other six days of the week—specifically to help others in some way—that really count.

I designed a simple road test to help readers experience what it's like to live a helpful lifestyle and join God in making the world a better place. This road test will help you confirm three important things:

- *How you feel about yourself when you live in this helpful way*: First, you can determine firsthand how such helpful activities make you feel. I'm confident you will feel good about each of the helpful things you do. However, it requires actually *doing* them, not just talking about them, to experience the feeling this lifestyle provides.

- *How other people react to your goodness*: Second, you can experience, again firsthand, how other people react to you when you use your life to help them in some way. There is no greater feeling than the one we have when someone sincerely thanks us for something meaningful we did for them.

- *How a helpful way of living can improve, even change, your life*: Third, you can determine how partnering with God and your Spirit of Goodness to help others changes or impacts your life. While we have referred to this as a road test, in reality these are real-life experiences of what happens when you respond positively to God's love signals and the helpful nudges your Spirit of Goodness provides.

Road Testing a Helpful Way of Living

I believe God has called us to live a helpful lifestyle in which we are concerned about others and their well-being. One of the nice things about this calling is that you can road test living this way to determine for yourself how it makes you feel and how others react when you behave as a more concerned and helpful individual. Here are five activities you can complete to test this way of living and see how a more helpful lifestyle might work for you:

- *Say something nice but unexpected to someone*: Whether at school, work, or elsewhere, we encounter people during our typical day who provide us with opportunities to be nice. It could be the person who bagged your groceries at the store or a student at school you met for the first time; it could be a neighbor whom you see now and then but have made no effort to speak to. We have dozens of opportunities every day to say "Thank you," or "How are you doing?" or "It's nice to see you." These may not be major moments in life, but they are still meaningful opportunities to share some goodness with another person.

- *Contact someone to tell them you were thinking about them*: Every one of us has friends or acquaintances we haven't seen in a long time. Possibilities might include fellow students from our high school or college years, a former neighbor when we lived in another city or different part of town, or even someone we met at church or a social function. Obviously, you have to handle such contacts in a polite and positive way, but you might be surprised by the reaction you receive from extending a hand (or email) of friendship to someone who wasn't expecting it.

- *Deliver a meal to someone older or in need*: This will take a special effort on your part because you will not only need to call them to get permission to bring the meal, but you'll have to cook it or buy it as well. While the food itself might be important to the recipients, it's the fact that you made a special effort to help them that will count the most.

- *Visit someone in a retirement community*: This will require some research and a few phone calls, but contact one or more of the retirement communities in your area to determine if there is a resident there who may be a bit lonely or without family and who would welcome a short visit. If you're successful in making such an arrangement, be sure to take some flowers or a small gift on your first visit. Hopefully, you'll be able to stop by for additional visits every week or so.

- *Volunteer to assist a local nonprofit or a special community program*: Nonprofits, churches, local governments, and other organized groups do important work, but they always need people to help. Do some homework and find one of these groups that interests you. Contact them to see how you might assist them for an afternoon, a day, or a weekend. The advantage here is that you have the opportunity to select a worthwhile work of goodness in which you could participate long term.

Expand This Road Test

I'm sure there are additional things you can identify and do for others to help you determine if living in this helpful way is something you should incorporate into your life. Adding five more activities of your own or doubling up on each of the above suggestions will help you make this a ten-step road test that is even more helpful to others and to yourself.

Another way to expand this road test is to do something helpful that you've been intending to do for some time, but for some reason you just haven't done yet. You've been thinking about it and planning to make the call, send the message, go see this person, or do some other helpful thing, but you have not made a firm choice to turn your intention into reality. Well, now is a great time to add this to your list and do it.

The Choice to Live This Way

If you decide you want to start living in this helpful way, you have everything you need to do so, including God's influence for spreading love and goodness in the world, your Spirit of Goodness to provide you with nudges when needed, and the thousands of people who yearn to feel more love and goodness in their lives. It then becomes a matter of deciding on the extent to which you will live in this helpful way.

"Try it; you'll like it," as the saying goes. And I bet you will.

It is not enough that we do our best;
sometimes we have to do what is required.

WINSTON CHURCHILL

Example 6

A LOVE AND GOODNESS STORY
Honesty Pays

No matter our circumstances or situation in life, we can be honest in our dealings with others. In this story, Freddy, a homeless man who had to beg on the street to get something to eat, passed up the opportunity to make $4,000 and instead did the honest thing.

Luck changed for Freddy one day when the usual tinkling of coins being dropped into his beggar's cup was punctuated by a slightly heavier clunk. A few minutes later, he looked inside and spied a woman's engagement ring with a diamond in it.

The first thought of a man begging to survive might have been to run to the nearest jewelry shop. And that was what Freddy did. But when he was offered $4,000 for the ring, a better instinct took charge as something inside made him feel that he was doing the wrong thing. So, he left the shop and kept the ring just in case the owner came back.

The owner returned two mornings later. Marybeth said she may have dropped something valuable into his cup.

"Was it a ring?" he asked.

"Yes, it was," she said.

"Well, I have it," Freddy replied.

With her husband, Marybeth decided to do something special for Freddy. They set up an online fund to raise the $4,000 that Freddy had turned down. The fund raised over $200,000. In addition, a sister with whom he had lost touch heard the story on the news and realized Freddy was her brother.

Whatever motivated Freddy to turn down the cash from the jeweler—he attributed it to the teachings of his pastor grandfather, who'd raised him—he was repaid. Six weeks later, he was reunited with long-lost siblings, and he had a home, a job, and enough money to give up begging.

Marybeth had started the fairy tale when she'd reached into her purse that day in February for coins, forgetting that amongst them was her diamond ring. "I thought for sure I would never get it back," she said.

We may not encounter a situation where such a valuable item is involved, but we have many opportunities every week to say the right thing or be honest. The next time you encounter such a moment, remember Freddy's story and conduct yourself as he did by doing or saying the right thing. You may not find your lost sister, but you will gain the respect of the people you interact with each day, and you will feel much better about yourself and the life you are living.

CHAPTER 7

THOSE ALL-IMPORTANT CHOICES

Opening Thought

No question, life comes with plenty of challenges. Some of these might include:

- financial resources that aren't what we need them to be.
- friends who try to influence us in questionable ways.
- family support that may be lacking.
- educational opportunities we misused or skipped completely.
- relationships that didn't work out.
- a bad choice we made years ago that still haunts us today.

Granted, some of these challenges are greater than others. But no one is immune to such difficulties. We all encounter circumstances that we have to work through and somehow overcome. The question is: How do we do it?

We start by making good choices and continuing to do so over an extended period of time. We do it by asking God to direct us as we set new goals and objectives and choose our way toward achieving them.

It may not be easy, it may take time, and it may seem that the odds are stacked against you. But if you're willing to make meaningful choices and back them diligently, you can achieve incredible things with your life. On the other hand, if you choose to wander along in life hoping that things will work out someday, you're unlikely to accomplish much.

To achieve significant results, you have to give your life some careful thought and make specific choices concerning what you want to achieve. While luck can be a factor in our circumstances, the primary ingredient in having a truly successful life is the extent to which we incorporate love and goodness into our choices.

It isn't how much you do that counts,
but how much you do well and how often you decide right.

WILLIAM FEATHER

God Has Equipped Us for This Work

I believe God has equipped us for the work we have to do to develop our life and manage it effectively. God has done many things for us. But these five things, all given to us by God, seem to be the most important:

- *The opportunity to live a life*: First, God gave us the life we have and the opportunity to experience life itself. Yes, your parents played an important role, but God blessed your life from moment one.

- *Love signals in our hearts to guide us*: Second, God's love has been given to us and continues to speak through our hearts, providing important signals for how we should live our lives.

- *A unique set of interests, abilities, and feelings*: Third, God blessed us with unique interests, abilities, and feelings to accomplish our purpose in life. And with God's help, these three qualities will lead us to that purpose.

- *Our Spirit of Goodness to help us make good choices*: Fourth, God has instilled our Spirit of Goodness in our lives to help us not only think through the choices we make but also arrive at a choice that is good for others as well as ourselves.

- *Special direction to people in need*: Fifth, God leads us to people and situations in need of the assistance that we can provide. In effect, God directs us to opportunities to use our lives for the good of others.

With all this support, you would think success and satisfaction would be foregone conclusions. However, we possess *the power of choice*, which means that it is ultimately up to us how we utilize our personal qualities, develop our abilities, and follow the guidance God provides.

Believing in God and recognizing our Spirit of Goodness are choices we make. Hopefully, they are choices we've thought about carefully and prayed about as well. Of all the important choices we make in life, in my opinion, accepting and believing in God is by far the most important. Not because it provides us with a "ticket to Heaven," but because it sets a loving and helpful tone for managing our lives and helps make our lives count for others, not just for ourselves.

> *Somewhere along the way, we must learn*
> *that there is nothing greater than to do something for others.*
>
> DR. MARTIN LUTHER KING JR.

The Power of Our Choices

We tend to grossly underestimate the power of our choices. We think our circumstances control us instead of believing that we can manage and modify our circumstances through the choices we make. Granted, there are some things in life we can't change. However, the fact remains that much of our life—and I would argue most of it—is defined by our personal choices.

Here are five key areas of life that are controlled and defined by the choices we make:

- *Our day-to-day activities*: Our choices determine what we will do today, this week, and in the future. The plans we make in life—short- and long-term—are executed through our personal choices.

- *Our character*: Our honesty, our helpfulness, our respect for others, our friendliness, and our general conduct and demeanor are all determined, defined, and exhibited by the choices we make.

- *Our relationships with others*: Chemistry is indeed a magic ingredient, but longer term, the depth of our relationships with others is almost totally defined by how we choose to treat them.

- *Our attitude about life and living*: Positive attitudes are not easy to come by, but we can all significantly improve our attitude if we accept that we are here to help others and set about to do that.

- *The objectives—short- and long-term—we have for our lives*: We must have objectives and goals we want to accomplish, but once identified, our choices determine our success in achieving them.

As mentioned in previous chapters, our choices define us, both today and in the future—so choose wisely.

Managing the power of choice,
with all its creative and spiritual implications,
is the essence of the human experience.
Choice is the process of creation itself.

CAROLINE MYSS

Helping Others: A Critical Choice

We can now add *goodness/helping others* to the list of the key areas above that are choice-dependent. Like the other five, the goodness your life imparts is controlled by your choices. I would encourage you to give sincere thought to your lifestyle and decide to what extent you want to use your life to help others. Granted, you may feel concerned about others from time to time, but the degree to which your life actually helps them depends on your choices and the actions you take as a result.

Why are our goodness-related choices so important? Simply stated, because they set in motion some of the most significant things we will ever do with our lives. There's no other feeling that comes close to the one we have when we know we have helped another individual in some special way.

Whoever in trouble or sorrow needs your help,
give it to them.
Whoever in anxiety or fear needs your friendship,
give it to them.
It isn't important whether they like you.
It isn't important whether you approve of their conduct.
It isn't important what their creed or nationality may be.
What's important is that you help.

E. N. WEST

Spiritual Guidance Improves Our Choices

Goodness and helping others starts with a special feeling of compassion, sympathy, or empathy inside us. It's a feeling of concern for someone in need. It's the desire to see their circumstances improve. It's the motivation to get up and do something to improve the situation and help someone have a better life. That compulsion to help pulls on us, but where does it come from? It seems totally logical to me that this motivation to do something helpful is God's love and our Spirit of Goodness at work within us.

As I've stated several times now, I believe God works primarily through people and motivates us to use our lives to help others. To me, it's a simple understanding, but it's possibly the most crucial one we will ever have. *Because once you realize God is at work in and through you, the importance of your life and how you live it multiplies significantly.*

However, our choices quickly take over and ultimately control what we say and do. If you respond to a feeling of God's love and choose to reach out and help someone in need, your life delivers the goodness that clearly started within. If, however, you make the choice to ignore such influences, you miss an opportunity to experience what life is really all about.

As you reflect on the importance of your choices and consider how you might increase the level of goodness your life imparts, there are two fundamental ideas I would encourage you to think about:

- *We are here for each other*: Probably the biggest mistake we make in managing our lives is focusing on ourselves, our needs, and our wants. While some of this is natural and necessary, we miss some of life's greatest and most rewarding experiences if we fail to balance our personal concerns with a sincere concern for others. We are not here to live just for ourselves, but to help others have better lives as well. If there is a simple secret to living a meaningful and fulfilling life, it's focusing on the needs of others.

- *No matter what, we can use our lives to help others*: No matter our past, our historical indifference toward others, or any mistakes we may have made, the opportunity to use our lives to help others remains intact. People may be indifferent toward us or turn away from us completely, but God remains with us. If we pay attention, God will signal opportunities to us to show concern for friends and neighbors, to improve our community in some special way, or to devote our lives to a work that would make the world a better place.

Helping others is the secret sauce to a happy life.

TODD STOCKER

You don't have to be a member of a church, synagogue, or special religious group to follow God's lead. You just have to make the choice to respond to the feelings (love signals) God provides within you. You already have everything you need: God is already speaking to your heart, your Spirit of Goodness is already with you, and God has equipped you with a unique set of interests, abilities, and feelings to utilize in your life. You just have to accept God's presence within you, pay attention to where it leads you, and make the choices that will get you there.

God's Influence, Our Choices, and Miracles

Like many of you, I have long sought to understand the relationship between how God works in the world and actual events. Simply having faith that it happens this way or that, as explained in many religious writings, didn't seem logical to me. So, a lot of my motivation to write this book was to explain—primarily to myself, but hopefully to others as well—how I believe God works in the world today.

I've concluded that there is a definite connection between God's love, our Spirit of Goodness, and the miracles we witness from time to time. There is this want-to-help feeling that most of us have about others, particularly those in need. I believe this feeling, this motivation, is God at work within us, motivating us to help others in special ways.

The term "miracle" has somehow been confined to describing almost unbelievable events. However, it seems to me miracles come in all shapes and sizes, and it's the positive impact that our words and actions have on someone that determines whether something is a miracle or not.

Yes, many of the major ones are handled by God directly. However, the majority of the miracles that take place each day start with God's loving influence in our hearts motivating us to help someone in some way. The delivery of that miracle is then subject to an actual choice—made by us—to do what God is calling us to do. This miracle work, as I see it, is the primary objective of our partnership with God. As such, I believe a miracle happens when . . .

- . . . someone makes another person feel better by doing something kind and helpful, even if it's in a small way.
- . . . someone gives an unhoused woman money to buy food for herself and her children.
- . . . someone at school stops a larger kid from bullying or picking on a smaller one.
- . . . a teacher helps a student understand a math problem and how to solve it.
- . . . a surgeon and their medical team complete hours of tedious surgery that saves a person's life.

It is through experiences like these that God—working through people like you, me, and others—performs millions of miracles throughout the world each day. Your life takes on a special meaning when you make the choice to join God in this miracle work.

The mystery of human existence
lies not in staying alive, but in finding
something to live for.

FYODOR DOSTOEVSKY

Example 7

A LOVE AND GOODNESS STORY
Goodness Saved the Day

Love and goodness can sometimes be conveyed by a group response to a certain need. Beth posted this on Facebook, sharing her experience as one member of a small group of women who came to the rescue of a young mom in need. Part of Beth's report is included below.

Something extraordinary happened at LAX today. I was at the gate, waiting to get on my plane to Memphis. Flights to two different cities were boarding on either side of the Memphis flight. A toddler who looked to be eighteen months old was having a total meltdown, running between the seats, kicking and screaming, then lying on the ground and refusing to board the plane.

His young mom, who was clearly pregnant and traveling alone with her son, became completely overwhelmed. She couldn't pick him up because he was so upset and kept running away from her, then throwing himself to the ground, kicking and screaming again. The mother finally sat down on the floor and put her head in her hands, her kid next to her still having a meltdown, and she started crying.

Then, this wonderful thing happened. The women in the terminal area—there must have been six or seven of us—approached and surrounded the mother and the little boy. We knelt down and formed a circle around them. I sang "The Itsy-Bitsy Spider" to the little boy. One woman peeled an orange, another had a toy in her bag that she let the toddler play with, and another woman gave the mom a bottle of water. Someone else helped the mom get the kid's sippy cup out of her bag and helped her give it to him.

It was so special. There was no discussion and none of us knew each other, but we were able to calm them both down, and she got her child on the plane. After they went through the door, we all went back to our separate seats and didn't talk about it. We were strangers, gathering to solve a human problem. I will never forget that moment.

As I have stated many times in this book, love is reflected in our feelings about someone and goodness is when we actually do *something to put those feelings into action. Most definitely, this group of women* did *so much more than just feel sorry for the young mother and tell others about it later. Good for them! They responded to their Spirits of Goodness and met the mother's need right then and there.*

CHAPTER 8

WHY ARE YOU HERE?

Opening Thought

You know you're here, but do you know why?

That may sound like a silly question, since most of us simply accept the fact that we're here without giving much serious thought as to why. However, I see many people using their lives to help others—great neighbors, wonderful teachers, talented accountants, capable builders, insightful ministers, and focused physical therapists, to mention only a very few. Many of these people seem to have a purpose for being as they go about their lives each day.

When talking with them, we find that most of these people had (and still have) something inside them that not only appears in their talents but also influences the way they have chosen to live their lives, much of which involves sharing their love and goodness—as well as their interests, abilities, and feelings—with others.

I believe God has called these individuals, as well as millions similar to them, through the love in their hearts to help with God's work here on earth. What a wonderful feeling to know that you are devoting your life to something that God wants and needs you to do.

*The purpose of life is to contribute in some way
to making things better.*

ROBERT F. KENNEDY

Sometimes We Wish for the Wrong Things

We've all wished we could be someone else—someone we think of as talented, or pretty, or smart, or wealthy. We watch the medals being awarded at the Olympics and find ourselves wishing for some of that glory. We watch the hit movie and wish we were the attractive actor on the big screen. Sometimes it's the person with two million YouTube followers whom we envy. We've all experienced feelings like these.

For some reason, we tend to think we need to achieve a certain level of fame and fortune to be important to those around us. As a result, we frequently focus on ourselves, including the things we have, how we dress, and what we have to do to win the approval of others.

We need a clearer understanding of why we're here.

Many of us fail to understand that living a meaningful and effective life is not just about us. It's almost entirely about how we use our lives to help others, how we make other people's lives better even in small ways.

Marcus Tullius Cicero, the Roman statesman and lawyer, gave us a key insight into the answer when he summarized it this way:

Non nobis solum nati sumus.
(Not for ourselves alone are we born.)

Adjusting Our Focus

Here is one fundamental understanding that can enhance our lives significantly: *Our lives were not given to us just for our personal enjoyment.* You are not here to live just for yourself, but also to use your life to help others. You are not here to *get* more, but to *give* more. Realizing

82

this can be a life-changer. When you adjust the focus of your life from exclusively helping *yourself* to also helping *others*, you change your life in a significant way.

You may think I'm splitting hairs here, but it's not simply our day-to-day activities that are important. What's essential is how we use those activities to help others in some way. For example, it's not that important that you're a banker; what matters is that you're a banker working to help others have a better life. It's not that important that you are a law-abiding neighbor; what's important is that you reach out to help your neighbor in need in some special way. It's not just what you *do*, but what you *do to help others* that is important.

Confirming your purpose—what God wants and needs you to do with your life given your interests, abilities, and feelings—is, of course, significant. But what also matters is the type of person you are, or turn out to be, and the extent to which you help others in some way. Helping others is *the important thing*, and if we are willing to make the right choices, every one of us can get the important thing right.

You Can Make People Feel Special

In your own unique way, you can make other people feel special and cared for, feel they matter. It's a caring that comes from your heart that is inspired by God's love within you as you reach out to improve the lives of others in some way. The act of giving ourselves to others is what makes us whole.

> *It is one of the most beautiful compensations of this life that no person can sincerely try to help another without helping themselves.*
>
> RALPH WALDO EMERSON

One of life's most critical insights is that we're not here for ourselves, but rather to help others have better lives even in small ways. In working to do so, we not only improve someone else's life, but we improve our lives as well. Just try it. Reach out and help someone in a special and sincere way. Not only will your actions make them feel better and let them know that someone cares about them, but you will feel something special in your life as well.

Life works in a way that's opposite to how we typically think. It's not really about helping ourselves that makes us successful. It's all about using our lives to help others. May more of us come to understand this valuable insight. After all, that's why we're here.

> *Love and kindness are never wasted.*
> *They always make a difference.*
> *They bless the one who receives them,*
> *and they bless you, the giver.*

> BARBARA DEANGELIS

Valuing Your Life's Purpose

You're here for a reason, but what is it? Accurately answering this question requires two things:

- *Understand that you were meant to be unique and different:* First, you have to believe that you were never intended to be like other people, but that you are unique and that you have a special role to play in your family, your community, and the world. You have to believe that you have *a special mission*, a calling if you will, if you're ever going to determine what it is.

- *Understand that your life has a special purpose:* Second, and more challenging, is to determine what your life's role is, or should be, and what you have to do to fulfill it. However, it's very difficult, if not impossible, to make this determination if you don't first believe that you have a special purpose, given to you by God, to help you make life better for others in some special way.

Even if you've wasted some important time or possibly made some mistakes that you regret, your life is still special, and if you so decide, you can do some very good things with it.

Determining Your Life's Purpose

I can't answer your purpose question for you, not even close, but I can help you make that determination for yourself. Here are four actions you can take to help you find and confirm the purpose of your life:

- *Focus on your interests, abilities, and feelings:* These gifts, given to you by God, hold much of the answer to your purpose question.

  Interests can appear early in life and offer the first signs of what is intended for you. When you detect an interest in some career or life role possibilities, don't stop there, but do some research about them. Here's where the internet can work to your advantage, allowing you to, in effect, travel the world and collect information about something that interests you.

  Abilities start with small things that you do well and that you like doing. For example, someone who enjoys working with numbers is more likely to be called into finance or accounting than to building or road construction. Think about the little things you like to do, as they can be big clues to what you are being called to do with your life.

  Feelings, especially strong ones, are important indications of what you are being called to do with your life, especially when they match up with one or both of the above. People who enjoy, even love, what they do are always more successful in helping others than those who feel otherwise.

- *Ask God to help you evaluate the three areas above:* This is especially important when you have identified something of value to you and are trying to determine what that value is saying to you. Pray to God at any time, and as often as you want, as you evaluate your options. Remember, God gave you these interests, abilities, and feelings in the first place, so there is no one better at helping you determine what they're saying to you.

- *Apply the love test to each option you are considering:* As you narrow down the options for your life's role or career, apply the love test to each of them. *Would I love doing this? Would I love going this route even though I know it will be challenging?* As stated above, people who love what they do are always more successful than those who don't.

- *Consider the goodness—helping others—your life would impart:* After all, that's why you're here: to help others have better lives and to help God make the world a little better as a result of the life you live. If you ever need a tiebreaker between alternatives that seem to be a great fit for you, let the amount of goodness your life would provide to others be the deciding factor.

So, why are we here? Without question, to use our lives in such a way that other people will live better because we were here. Let that objective remain at the top of your list every day that you are fortunate enough to live the life God has provided for you.

> *What our deepest self craves is not mere enjoyment,*
> *but a supreme purpose that will enlist all our powers*
> *and give unity and direction to our life.*

HENRY J. GOLDING

All New Lives Are Blessed by God

Regardless of the circumstances of our childhood, I believe each of us is intended to be here and is blessed by God with a definite purpose for our lives.

Whether your parents were just casual friends "playing around" or a committed married couple who had no plans to have another child, every one of us starts our life journey with God's blessing. For reasons we may never understand, God had intentions for the union that created us, and as proof, God blessed it with a new life. What matters is that this new life is given the opportunity to become the person God intends and plans for it to be.

When a child is allowed to develop and grow, special interests, abilities, and feelings reveal themselves at an early age, and a unique individual emerges. Not long after, this young person starts to express themselves in specific ways concerning what they want—and are being led—to do with their lives.

I believe these personal qualities are God-given and evidence of God shaping the life of a developing young person to become a physician, a teacher, a pastor, a scientist, a special friend, a great neighbor, a builder, a lawyer, or one of thousands of other roles that are needed in the world today. With the support and guidance of parents, this new life will someday share its love and goodness and make a difference in the lives of others.

That said, here are some sad but true statistics. According to the Pew Research Center, each year over one million potential new lives in the United States are not given the opportunity to live the life that God has given to them. The World Health Organization reports that there are over seventy-three million new lives worldwide that are terminated prior to birth each year. I can't believe God is very happy about this, given the intentions God had for these lives.

Yes, it's a tough job raising a child and giving it the opportunity to develop into a responsible adult, but that is exactly what God calls parents to do. God has given them the responsibility of sharing their love, goodness, and guidance with this new life and helping it develop into the special individual that God is calling it to be. It's left to the parents to *make the choice* whether they will accept their God-given responsibility to raise their child or not.

Let's Be Honest About Fairness Here

We fight so hard for fairness and equal opportunities these days, but what could be fairer than to give someone the opportunity to live their life? What could be more important than to give a developing human being the opportunity to become the person God intended them to be? It doesn't make sense to me why anyone would fight for fairness and equal opportunities for individuals *who are already in this world* and not do exactly the same for those individuals *who soon will be.*

You Could Help Save a Life

There are many mothers-to-be who don't have the needed support from their families or partners to help them through their pregnancy and assist in finding a home for their baby. The mother-to-be might also be embarrassed by her circumstances. As a result, ending the pregnancy seems the most logical solution.

However, if they had the love and goodness of a caring individual, many would work through their issues and bring their child into this world. Given that there are between one and two million couples in the United States waiting to adopt, the challenge is to help the new mother through the birth, and if she so decides, through the adoption process as well.

If you feel called to help someone in these circumstances, I urge you to ask God to guide you and then find someone who would benefit from your love and assistance. There are nonprofits involved in this work, so you might start there. Certainly, the internet might lead you to someone with such needs. Church staff are often able to assist in identifying someone needing such help.

If you make the choice to help in this way, you will be working to save someone's life, someone who someday may play an important role in the lives of others and in making the world a better place for everyone. I can think of no more important love and goodness work than this.

> *How many physicians, scientists, teachers, pastors,*
> *missionaries, musicians, businesspeople, and*
> *notable contributors to society*
> *have been murdered in the womb?*

CHUCK BALDWIN

Example 8

A LOVE AND GOODNESS STORY

Family Goodness

It's generally expected that certain days of the year are times to focus on our families and enjoy being with them. Thanksgiving, Christmas, and birthdays fall into this category. Here is an example where parents wanted to help their children learn the importance of thinking about others, of sharing love and goodness with others, even on special days like these.

The emergency room was jammed on Christmas Day 2022. Patients poured in post-pandemic with upper respiratory diseases, some related to coronavirus, the flu, and other ailments. The thirty-bed emergency room had at least seventy patients that day. More than two dozen staffers were on duty, feverishly working to provide care.

That afternoon, Pete, his wife, and their two children arrived at the hospital's emergency room with twenty-five freshly baked pizzas. This act of goodness made the day extra special for the hardworking staffers.

"What a selfless act," said the chief of emergency medicine at the hospital. "This family brought us twenty-five pizzas!"

Pete knew the staff would be working hard and wanted to show his appreciation for their efforts by feeding those who couldn't be with their families. Together with his wife, two children, and visiting relatives, they worked to bake the pizzas after opening their presents.

Pete explained that he and his wife are teaching their children about giving back to the community. "We want to teach them that the holiday is not all about getting gifts," he said. "It's about sharing with others. They know it's for a good cause."

"It feels good to know you did something to help others," Pete's eleven-year-old son said. "They [the hospital staff] were working all day."

Pete's wife said the hospital workers were so happy when they saw the pizzas. She noted that the staff had been snacking on cookies when the pizzas arrived.

The staff couldn't thank the family enough, and Pete's children learned something very important that day.

Several things about this story are memorable and provide teaching moments for us all. However, the thing I noticed most was what Pete's son said about the experience: "It feels good to know you did something to help others."

His comment is a testimony to something mentioned several times in this book: Just thinking about someone in need is not enough; you have to actually do something helpful to experience what goodness is all about. If you are a parent, I urge you to organize a similar activity in which your family can do something together that will help others in some special way.

CHAPTER 9

LIVING WITH GOODNESS

Opening Thought

This is a sad but true story.

As I ate lunch by myself one day while catching up on the news, a story popped up on my phone about a sixteen-year-old girl who had just committed suicide. She'd been going through a very stressful period in her life and had posted a question on social media asking: "Really important, help me choose D/L." The D/L meant death or life. Surprisingly, over 70 percent of the girl's acquaintances replied "D." Upon seeing the results, the girl went out and jumped off the roof of a nearby building.

I couldn't help but wonder why more people didn't reach out and try to help her instead of responding the way they did. How much effort would it have taken to send a message of concern or simply ask: *What can I do to help you?* How much time would it have taken for these so-called friends to show they cared about this girl and were there to support her in any way they could? No doubt, things would have turned out differently, and she might be alive today if those individuals had responded in a more helpful way.

*No greater burden can be borne by an individual
than to know no one cares or understands.*

ARTHUR H. STAINBACK

We Have Choices Concerning How We Treat Others

We do have choices about how we treat others. We can choose to be positive and helpful, *or* we can respond to people in sarcastic, even hurtful ways. We can choose to reach out and help someone we know who has a problem and needs someone to show that they care, *or* we can let it go and not worry about them. We can choose to stand up for someone who is being bullied, *or* we can ignore the situation and walk away. In other words, how we react to the needs of others is a *choice* we make several times each day.

We may think that, in the grand scheme of things, little choices like these are no big deal. We may even think a sharply worded text message won't really hurt the recipient's feelings. But that's poor thinking. Moments like these and the opportunities they present are, in fact, what living with goodness is all about.

*We are not here on earth to see through each other;
we are here to see each other through.*

GLORIA VANDERBILT

God Equips Us to Help Each Other

In effect, our unique interests and abilities allow us to do special things for each other: to heal, teach, feed, transport, and help each other in many different ways. Our differences allow us to support each other and provide us with the opportunity to find and receive the assistance we need.

If you agree that our differences work for the collective good, the next question is: *Where do our unique interests, abilities, and feelings come from?* Clearly, some portion of them develops from what we learn from other people, from school, or from our experiences. *But how did the seeds of these interests, abilities, and feelings get planted in us in the first place?*

This last question is the crucial one. My personal belief—and the longer I live, the stronger this belief has become—is that our interests and abilities are God-given. As such, it's logical for me to see and understand that God works in this world primarily through people—individuals like you and me—to heal, teach, feed, and help people in many, many ways. I believe the primary reason we are here is to carry out God's work in the world and to help each other have better lives.

That's all well and good, you say, but why do some people show little or no concern for others? Why do some of us live in selfish ways? Why do some people even harm others? This is another important question: *Why do people act in these detrimental ways?*

The answer is this: *Because they refuse to acknowledge that the basic purpose of their lives is to help others, and as a result, they make self-ish choices instead of helpful ones.* In an earlier chapter, we addressed the relationship between choices and goodness and how our lives are shaped and defined by the choices we make. We can make the choice to work out our lives on our own, or we can choose to follow where our interests, abilities, and feelings may lead. We can choose to ignore our Spirit of Goodness within us and live however we want, or we can make the choice to identify our God-given purpose and help others in some special way. Deciding which of these ways you will live is one of the most important choices you will ever make.

Lord, make me an instrument of thy peace.
Where there is hatred, let me sow love;
where there is injury, pardon;
where there is doubt, faith;

where there is despair, hope;
where there is darkness, light;
and where there is sadness, joy.

PRAYER BY FRANCIS OF ASSISI

Traveling with Our Uniqueness

If we make the choice to use our interests, abilities, and feelings—our God-given uniqueness, if you will—to help others, it becomes the beginning of a journey. It's a choice that frames our life and provides us with a key objective: to use our lives to improve the lives of others. It's a choice that activates our lives in positive ways and points us in a direction that will, over time, allow us to improve the world in our own special way. I have characterized this as *living with goodness.*

What does *living with goodness* really mean? Here are the main characteristics of choosing to live our lives in this goodness-oriented way:

- *It means treating others with respect*: That other person is unique too. They have the opportunity to *live with goodness* as well. Depending on their choices, they have the opportunity to find their intended purpose and help others in their own special way. Therefore, we should always have respect for them and the life journey they may be on.

- *It means making life better for others*: Wherever we are—at home, school, work, or within our community—we should continually work to make life better for others, whether our choice has a large impact, only makes a small improvement in someone's life, or simply shows someone you care. Every helpful choice counts.

- *It means focusing on our interests, abilities, and feelings to determine how God intends us to live our lives*: It's not likely that you will fully understand what these life-definers are saying to you or how they are directing your life on day one. Therefore, as we *live with goodness*, we must continue to work to understand what is intended for our life and how we should live it.

- *It means supporting an important issue or cause*: Yes, we need to take care of the home front first, but as we *live with goodness*, we should look for at least one citywide, countrywide, or worldwide effort to join that might make life better for others—friends and enemies alike.

- *It means being willing to be there when someone with special needs or circumstances appears in our lives*: In your life, you will encounter people within your reach with special needs. *Living with goodness* means helping to make things better for them however you can.

Distractions Along the Way

These distractions are often referred to as temptations. They are things in life that tempt or motivate us to say or do things we shouldn't. Over the years, we've tended to give the devil credit for exposing us to such things and leading us off in some bad direction. But in fact, many of these temptations are everyday motivations—how we want to dress, the car we want to drive, the phone we want to have, or even the text message we want to send. Not that these things don't have some level of importance in our lives, but when we let them take priority, they can cause us to totally miss the way we were intended to live our lives.

Bottom line: It takes a wise person to make the choice to *live with goodness* and see the value of living their life for others instead of simply living it for themselves. It takes a wise person to make the choice to put themselves second and prioritize the well-being of others. It takes a wise person to realize their unique capabilities are leading them to be of service to others and to the world. It takes a wise person to see that simple goodness is disappearing from the world and that we need more people who will take a stand for goodness and work to motivate others to make the same choice. You can be such a person.

Yes, Little Bits of Goodness Count

Whether it's something you say, something you text, or something small you do to help someone, little bits of goodness count. You never know when a few kind words, a small helpful gesture, or a positive text will lift someone's spirit and cause them to feel better about themselves or their circumstances. Living with goodness means using your choices—and your life—to make others' lives a little better.

Humans are powerful spiritual beings meant
to create good on earth.
This good isn't usually accomplished in bold actions
but in singular acts of kindness between people.
It's the little things that count, because they are
more spontaneous and show who you truly are.

DANNION BRINKLEY

I conclude this chapter by referring back to the sixteen-year-old girl who committed suicide as a result of over 70 percent of her social media "friends" texting the "D" option back to her. Clearly, those responders had never made *living with goodness* a priority in their lives and did not view themselves as having an important role to play in helping others have better lives.

To help all of us and to ensure that this young person did not die in vain, I hold her up in this book as a real-life circumstance of why we should all make sharing goodness a priority in our lives. You and your life touch the lives of many individuals every day. The more *love* and *goodness* you share with others during these encounters, the better and more rewarding your life, and theirs, will be.

All the other pleasures in life seem to wear out,
but the pleasure of helping someone never does.

JULIUS ROSENWALD

Example 9

A LOVE AND GOODNESS STORY

Chasing Loneliness Away

In our day-to-day lives, there are moments when we get to decide whether we want to offer a helping hand or word or let the circumstances pass. Such gestures often feel trivial to us, but they can have the power to change the course of someone's life. This kind of transformative experience happened to Bill when he was fifteen years old.

It was the fall of 1972, and Bill was attending a reunion for a summer program he'd taken part in a few months before. He was standing outside at the end of the day, catching up with friends. Eventually, everyone said their goodbyes, and Bill was left standing there by himself.

"Sometimes when you're alone, it's okay," Bill said. "But sometimes you feel abandoned. And that's the way I felt then." Nearby, another group of teenagers stood laughing and talking. "I found myself wishing so much to be a part of that other group," he said.

One of the people in the other group was a girl named Wendy. She and Bill had only met in passing at the summer program a few months earlier. As Bill stood there feeling increasingly lonely, Wendy noticed. She stepped away from her group, came up to him, and asked, "Would you like to join us?"

"Hard to believe, but my life was transformed in that moment," Bill said.

Wendy's reaching out sparked a realization in Bill: He could offer that same kindness to anyone, at any time.

"It's so easy to see someone who seems left out and alone and notice them, say hello to them, and be kind to them," Bill explained. "And my realization was that kindness is a gift we can all give."

Bill went on to become a psychiatrist. A primary part of his job is being kind to his patients, listening to them, and being attentive to their needs. Bill attributes much of his understanding of the importance of kindness to that moment with Wendy when he was fifteen years old.

"To the extent that I'm a good person in my life today, it's due in great part to Wendy inviting me to join her group that day," he said.

We tend to do our thing and leave it to others to do theirs. But almost every day, we encounter people and have the opportunity to greet and possibly talk to someone. Your willingness to take a sincere interest in the other person will not only benefit that person but will also contribute to you becoming a better person as well. Love and goodness don't always come in big buckets. Many times, it's the small sharing of a love and goodness moment that has the greatest impact on another person.

CHAPTER 10

HATE VERSUS LOVE AND GOODNESS

Opening Thought

These days, we're exposed to hate at almost every turn. On a daily basis, we read about shootings, killings, and robberies, hear derogatory comments made by politicians about fellow lawmakers, encounter negative postings on social media, and witness hateful texts sent by others. We may not notice it, but this abundance of hate is taking its toll on us. If we don't stop and think about what is happening and start working to increase the level of love and goodness coming from our lives, we are likely to become just another hater who does little actual good with their life.

Hate has caused a lot of problems in the world
but hasn't solved one yet.

MAYA ANGELOU

Hate Is Doing a Number on Us

We worry about a lot of things that might happen in the *future*, but we don't seem to be that concerned about the hate that is destroying our country and the world *today*. We worry about the spread of nuclear capabilities around the world, but we don't seem willing to address the hate crimes and drive-by shootings that take place in our cities every day. We are quick to point out politicians who we think are leading us in the wrong direction, but we don't seem willing to take a closer look at ourselves to determine how hate is causing us to say or do improper things. We readily accept the hateful texts that come our way and often join in with similar responses.

We seem to think we have a right to hate. We seem to believe we can be the judge and jury about anything or anyone who comes within our mental target range. It can be about one of our family members, or close friends, or someone we don't even know who lives thousands of miles away. We don't really care; if we don't like what someone is saying or doing—or even what they look like—we won't hesitate to release our hateful feelings and fire away.

Because hate takes place almost entirely within us, there are no hate police to pull us over and give us a ticket so that we will remember to slow down and do better next time. As a result, we tend to offer expressions of hate as substitutes for doing the harder job of understanding the person or circumstances involved. If we aren't careful, hate can cause us to make some terrible choices and use our lives to the detriment of others.

By its very nature, hate destroys and tears down.
By its very nature, love creates and builds up.

DR. MARTIN LUTHER KING JR.

Hate Seems to Be Everywhere

Unfortunately, our hate problem is not getting better. It is, in fact, getting worse and can now be found in almost every facet of our lives:

- *In online exchanges*: A January 2021 Pew Research Center survey found that 41 percent of Americans have been personally subjected to harassing (hateful) behavior online, and an even larger share (66 percent) have witnessed these behaviors directed at others. Further, a majority of Americans (62 percent) view online harassment as a major problem. *When people get online, their willingness to curb their hate toward others diminishes significantly.*

- *In our schools*: Bullying, which is an expression of hate, is a significant problem in almost every school. According to bullyingstatistics.org, more than 40 percent of children have been bullied online, and more than 160,000 children skip classes each day because of the fear of being bullied. According to an October 2024 Bureau of Justice Statistics report, 46 percent of males and 26 percent of females have been victims of physical bullying by other students. *No question, unbridled hate is resulting in physical attacks and harassment toward many of our young people today.*

- *In our country*: Hate crimes are defined as "crimes that manifest evidence of prejudice based on race, gender or gender identity, religion, disability, sexual orientation, or ethnicity," according to the Hate Crime Statistics Act passed by Congress in 1990. Hate crimes can be committed against people, property, or society and can include violent attacks and robbery, as well as arson and vandalism. The FBI reported 11,862 incidents of hate crimes in 2023 (the highest number ever recorded and up from 7,120 incidents in 2018). *Clearly, severe hate is on the rise in this country.*

- *In our politics and our media*: The political leaders of our country set poor examples by taking verbal shots at anyone they disagree with, and they reinforce their sentiments with frequent "gotcha" tweets. Politicians don't hesitate to say hateful things about someone who sees things differently than they do. Journalists repeat such hateful comments, often embellishing them to give them more bite, and broadcast them 24/7. James Antle III writes this on the subject:

> *There is a sickness in our political climate. Nearly two decades into our status as a 50-50 country, split into red states and blue states, many people on both sides of the political divide have literally begun to hate each other.*

- *In you and me*: Let's be honest here. You and I are part of the hate problem as well. Whether it's a neighbor who doesn't keep his yard mowed, a family member who consistently rubs us the wrong way, or someone at work or school who takes credit for an idea that's not truly theirs, we can quickly muster thoughts of hate about someone near us and nurse those hateful thoughts for an extended period of time. *Each and every one of us needs to do better.*

In short, the hate train has left the station and is winding its way through every town and city in this country, boarding more and more people with hate in their hearts about something or someone. We've got to find a meaningful way to slow down this hate train, maybe even stop it altogether, so that those on board can get off and find ways to replace their hate with words and actions that will improve their lives and the lives of those around them. Yes, it's hard to stop a train, but the better we understand how hate works, the better the chance we have of stopping the hate coming from our lives and never getting on board again.

Hate Is Really a Choice We Make

There are countless reasons why people hate:

- political differences
- sexual orientation or preferences
- racial differences

- envy of success or good fortune
- inappropriate personal conduct
- offending words or statements
- personality differences
- envy of clothing or electronic possessions

And on we go.

It can be helpful to understand why you have hateful feelings in your life. But to truly understand hate and how it works, we must look beyond the things or circumstances like those listed above. Instead, we must look at ourselves and what's going on inside us. It's not these "things" that cause us to hate, but rather our inability to control our reaction to them. In effect, *hate is an internal choice* we make in reaction to something we find challenging or offensive in some way.

The one good thing about hateful moments really being *choices* is that we can coach ourselves to stay neutral and make a better choice—a choice to conduct ourselves in a more mature way. Not necessarily to agree with the person or circumstance that triggered our hateful condition, but to respect others as individuals with different views when we encounter one of these hate-fueling moments. By doing so, we stop the hate train and give ourselves the opportunity to get off and move beyond our hateful feelings to something much better.

No one is born hating another person because
of the color of their skin,
or their background, or their religion.
People must learn to hate, and if they can learn to hate,
they can learn to love, for love comes more naturally
to the human heart.

NELSON MANDELA

How Do We Stop Hate?

Stopping hate is an important and worthwhile objective. But how do we actually do it? How do we minimize and hopefully eliminate the expressions of hate that seem to fester within us as we go about our daily lives? This may be one of the most crucial questions we ever ask ourselves. So, it's important that we take some time to consider not only our answer, but beyond that, what we can do to reduce or eliminate hate from our lives.

I offer you three ideas to focus on as you work to better understand how to reduce the hate coming from your life. Remember, I already pointed out that hate takes place inside or within us. Therefore, if we're going to fix our hate problem, we have to focus on what's going on inside us. As you work to live in a less hateful way, I suggest you reflect on these three things:

#1. Reflect on the Goodness Coming from You

I suggest that you start your personal eliminate-hate process by reflecting on the term "goodness" and where this internal ingredient comes from. Almost every one of us, at various times, feels a desire to help someone in some way, to say or do something that will improve someone's life. Such feelings are the opposite of hate. So, stop and ask yourself: *Where does our motivation to do something good for someone come from?*

I believe that God's love signals and our Spirit of Goodness are within each and every one of us and work in the world through people to help those in need in some way. Whether it's the medical team member who works to develop a much-needed vaccine, or the neighbor who takes dinner to the elderly shut-ins down the street, or the teachers who double their efforts to help their students understand a math problem, I see such helpful actions as God at work to help people have better lives. One way to define or label these helpful actions is with the term *living with goodness*, which in my view means teaming up with God and the Spirit of Goodness within you to make the world a better place.

Whether you have ever stopped to think about this or not, you have a role to play in helping spread goodness to those around you. You're not here to hate; you're here to make your family, friends, community, and the world better in some way. And, yes, I believe God works through individuals like you and me to spread goodness to as many people as possible.

> *Live in such a way that if people should see you,*
> *they could see God's goodness in you.*

ANONYMOUS

#2. Reflect on the Goodness Coming from Others

While this might be hard to accept, the target of our hate—the person(s) who said or did something that triggered the hateful feeling within us—has potential goodness within them too. Like you and me, God and their Spirit of Goodness are at work within them to motivate them to do good and helpful things for others as well, even if their current choices don't reflect this. Therefore, we should always be ready to temper our reactions to individuals we disagree with in order to make way for their goodness to come forth, now or in the future.

Yielding to someone we disagree with is always difficult, but keep in mind that it might be you or I who is seeing or believing things in the wrong way. By controlling our hate and not allowing ourselves to overreact to something, we create an opportunity to learn, grow, or at the very least, better understand the words or actions (choices) coming from the other individual.

> *Life becomes easier and more beautiful*
> *when we can see the good in other people.*

ROY T. BENNETT

#3. Reflect on the Need for More Goodness in the World

As I pointed out earlier, there is a tremendous need for more goodness in this world. In our online exchanges, in our schools and businesses, in our politics, in our media, and in you and me, this world needs more *love* and *goodness* on the part of everyone, no exceptions. And, while you and I might not have the power to change the world, we do have the power to show more love for one another, and as difficult as it may be, to eliminate the hate in our lives.

> *Each person has inside a basic decency and goodness.*
> *If they listen to it and act on it,*
> *they are giving a great deal of what it is the world needs most.*
> *It is not complicated, but it takes courage.*
> *It takes courage for a person to listen to their own goodness*
> *and act on it.*

PABLO CASALS

A Small Amount of Goodness Can Make a Big Difference

In researching simple but important acts of goodness for this section, I found hundreds of examples I could have used here, including:

- the man who missed his train to help an elderly lady with her bags so she could catch hers;

- the woman who secretly bought a stranger a set of badly needed truck tires he couldn't afford;

- the person who gave his Kindle to a homeless man who had been reading the same book over and over;

- the cleaners with the sign out saying, "If you are unemployed and need an outfit cleaned for an interview, we will clean it for free"; and

- the store employee who bent down to tie an elderly shopper's shoe so he wouldn't trip and fall.

However, there was one act of *love* and *goodness* that stood out among all of these. It was a poor man who had almost no worldly possessions who stopped his old, beat-up bicycle, got off, and gave his sandals to a young homeless girl who had no shoes. I thought, *If that poor man can give his only pair of sandals to this child, surely you and I can find ways to reveal our Spirit of Goodness by choosing to help those in need in some way.* May it be so for you and for me.

Will You Help or Hurt?

As stated several times in this book, when you help someone, even in a small way, you make the world a little better by the positive thing you say or do. The flipside of this is that when you hate someone, particularly if your words and actions reflect that hate, you make the world a little worse.

Unfortunately, we are currently experiencing a "sinking society"— a collective condition in which thoughts and actions toward others are getting worse, not better, as a result of the hate that has become a part of so many people's lives. It is critical for each of us to turn away from any hate in our lives and start getting our lives' directions from the love signals God provides.

Find the goodness that is already within you.

ECKHART TOLLE

Hate Versus Goodness: One More Point

Hate versus goodness: You have to work at managing which of these two will be the larger influence in your life. And remember, *one always pushes out the other.* In other words, the more hate you harbor within you or exhibit toward others, the less room you will have for love and goodness in your life.

The more you reveal hate in your words, deeds, or thoughts, the less inclined you will be to respond to God's love in your heart or to the motivations of your Spirit of Goodness to help others in some special way. You have to make the choice—whether you'll be a person who allows hate to be present in your life or a person *living with goodness*, making a conscious effort to help others as you go about your daily life.

You have an essential role to play in your family, your community, and in the world today. You may not have given that role much thought, but you are here for a reason. As one older but insightful lady told me, "You can be whoever you came here to be."

You have certain interests, abilities, and feelings about others that not only make you a unique individual but also point you to your calling in life. While finding your way to what is intended for you is no easy task, I can assure you of one thing: You will never find your true role in life through hate. It is only through *love* and *goodness* that you will become equipped to make this determination.

> *It is better to give love. Hatred is a low and degrading emotion and is so poisonous that no person is strong enough to use it safely. The hate we think we are directing against some person or thing has a devilish way of turning back upon us. When we seek revenge, we administer a slow poison to ourselves. When we administer caring and affection, it is astonishing what magical results we obtain.*

THOMAS DREIER

Example 10

A LOVE AND GOODNESS STORY

Small Gift, Big Results

This is another story where a person who wanted to help someone in a small way had a much bigger and lifelong impact on many more people. This proves once again that you can never tell what sharing a small amount of love and goodness today might grow into tomorrow.

Hilde Back was living in Nazi Germany when a stranger helped her escape to Sweden. As a Jewish woman in Germany, she had not been allowed an education. However, after she moved to Sweden, she was able to get a good education and eventually became a schoolteacher.

While a schoolteacher in Sweden, Hilde decided to confidentially sponsor one child's education in Kenya as a way of giving back something that had been given to her. After some research, she made the choice to sponsor Chris, a young man in Africa, at a cost of $15 per month.

Most poor children in Kenya cannot afford to pay secondary school tuition. Unfortunately, without an education, an extremely difficult and impoverished life is practically guaranteed. Thanks to Hilde's generosity, Chris avoided that fate.

Chris wound up graduating high school, going to the University of Nairobi, and then attending Harvard Law School. He became a UN human rights advocate and started a charity. He petitioned the Swedish embassy to find the name of his anonymous sponsor. Then he named his nonprofit the Hilde Back Education Fund (HBEF) after the benefactor he never met.

HBEF pays tuition for deserving poor students in Kenya. Since the charity's start, over one thousand children have been supported. Over one thousand lives have been changed so far. That doesn't even include the impact on their families. And who knows how many of these students will be inspired, as Chris was, to give back?

When talking about his background, Chris said, "I had very humble beginnings, growing up in a village that epitomized poverty: no paved roads, no electricity, no piped water, no medical facilities, and not much hope for a future. The school I went to did not have glass on its windows, none of us wore shoes, and most families had to endure hard labor in the coffee plantations to get insignificant sums of money to buy necessities. Many children did not have enough to eat at home."

And when talking about why he started HBEF to educate poor children, he said, "I think I want to see a world in which children have equal opportunity and are not robbed of their future by poverty, like so many of my friends in the village were."

It's interesting that the only reason Hilde was even alive to support Chris was because of a stranger's kindness. Both her parents were killed in concentration camps, but a stranger helped her escape.

This wonderful story about Hilde and Chris is a reminder that we can all make a difference, and you never know how big an impact your small act of love and goodness might have.

Clearly, Hilde significantly improved a lot of lives by making the choice (there's that do something *again) to help one person in a small way. I do believe that God has a way of multiplying our efforts if we take the first step. The needs in this world are great. If you feel the motivation to share some of your love and goodness with others, you can find plenty of people— nearby and far away—who can use it.*

CHAPTER 11

LABEL LESS AND LOVE MORE

Opening Thought

This is one of our biggest faults: judging people when we don't really know them. I don't know why we feel qualified to make such judgments, but it's one of the poorer choices we can make. If we're going to sign up for having more love and goodness coming from our lives, this is one of the first things we need to change.

We can see people who are not very attractive, or significantly overweight, or dressed in an unappealing way. While we may not give this person a specific label, we are quick to think less of them and conclude they are not someone we would like to meet. We make these types of shallow judgments several times each day when we don't know a single thing about the person or their background. Yet many times, the real person underneath all that is a smart, friendly, conversant, and talented individual.

You and I have to train ourselves to remain neutral in our thinking about someone based on superficial observations and hold our opinion until we get to know more about who they are and what's inside them. God values us based on what's inside. We should do the same when valuing others.

I am not what you see.
I am what time and effort and interaction slowly unveil.

RICHELLE E. GOODRICH

We Can Be Real People-Labeling Machines

At times, many of us operate as people-labeling machines. We tend to group people based on external factors and then—mistakenly— consider any member of that group to be like all the others. One of the biggest categories we use to label people is ethnicity. We group people based on the color of their skin or on some special clothing they wear. Whatever opinion we have of the group, right or wrong, carries over to the person in front of us, even though we know nothing else about them.

Religious labels are another way we separate people into groups. We may not even fully understand our own religion, yet we'll "doom someone to Hell" just because their beliefs are different from our own.

Sexuality is another label we use to classify people. It's none of our business, but we'll comment about someone's sexual orientation anyway. And of course, we label people based on their political group—we claim something's wrong with someone if they don't see the role of government as we do.

And We Don't Even Know Them

It's amazing when you stop and think that we can form our entire opinion about someone based on these labels. We can judge someone without having met them or talked with them face to face. We may say that we agree with the age-old teaching "Judge not that you be not judged," but we fail to practice it in our daily lives.

Almost every one of us is guilty of this type of ill-informed preju- dice to some degree. But regardless of why we do this, labeling people is a poor choice. It is much better to be an independent thinker and view people based on their individual characteristics, their personal conduct, and how they treat those around them.

It's time we make the choice to look at all people as unique individuals capable of loving, caring, wanting, and working just like you and me. We have to remind ourselves that those around us may look different and be different, but most people want the exact same things: to have an enjoyable and comfortable life and accomplish something meaningful and worthwhile.

It's what's inside a person that really counts. We simply need to stop being judgmental and pigeonholing people based on the way they look, how they talk, or what they believe. Today would be a good day to put your people-labeling machine away and never use it again.

> *Judging prevents us from understanding a new truth.*
> *Free yourself from the rules of old judgments*
> *and create the space for new understanding.*
>
> STEVE MARABOLI

What's Really Important Here?

So, what's really important in forming our opinion of someone?

There are many factors that come to bear on our view of another person, but the most important should be this: *How do they treat other people?* Are they nice, courteous, and helpful toward others? Never mind that he's a great football player—*how does he treat other people?* Never mind that she is very attractive—*how does she treat other people?* Never mind that he is successful in business—*how does he treat other people?* If someone treats other people in good, kind, and helpful ways, it's almost guaranteed they are good, kind, and helpful as well.

Let's quit judging people based on some label we place on them. Let's work harder at *loving* instead of *labeling*. Let's first evaluate ourselves to see if we're treating others with kindness and respect—with love and goodness. After we accomplish that, we can then evaluate others on the same basis—whether they are good and kind toward others as well. Clearly, we can use more good and kind people in this world. That's a label we should all be proud to wear.

Three things in human life are important:
the first is to be kind;
the second is to be kind; and the third is to be kind.

HENRY JAMES

Positive or Negative?

Are you a person who is generally positive? Do you frequently take note of the good things in life and say nice and supportive things about people around you? Or are you a negative individual frequently pointing out the wrongs in people or things that you don't like or are against? Clearly, life requires us to walk both sides of this street, but you know what I'm asking here. Would others classify you as primarily a positive or a negative individual?

This is important because negative people—people who are frequently pointing out the wrongs in others—don't accomplish as much in life as positive ones. There are two primary reasons for this. First, people don't like being around those who frequently point out the faults of others. We just don't enjoy being with people like that or want to include them in social gatherings or business ideas. Second, you only make progress in life when you focus on the good in others or on an idea that is good for others as well as yourself.

So, take stock of yourself and adjust your attitude and words as needed. If you're having trouble making this assessment, ask two of your good friends to confidentially share their *positive* versus *negative* assessment of you. This can be life-improving information, so don't shy away from getting an accurate reading. It can help you get in shape to share more love and goodness with the life that has been given to you.

*The greatest revelation of our generation
is the discovery that human beings,
by changing the inner attitudes of their minds,
can change the outer aspects of their lives.*

WILLIAM JAMES

Beware of the Influence of the Internet

If you are serious about becoming a kinder person and sharing more love and goodness with others, you have to consider how the information coming through the phone in your hand is conditioning you to be *more sarcastic, less caring,* and *increasingly inconsiderate* of others. Whether it's those texts that take shots at people, or the news headlines that are outright critical without all the facts, or the videos that humiliate others in the name of being funny, most of us encounter many of these types of conditioning moments each day.

If we're not careful, the day-in and day-out exposure to such information will train us to communicate in negative ways and words as well. When we do this, we become increasingly sarcastic, leaving less room in our day to show our caring and concern for other people. If you feel that you need to label less and love more, step back, honestly assess the quality of your communications with others, and determine what changes or adjustments you need to make.

*Information technology and the internet are rapidly
transforming every aspect of our lives—
some for better, but much for worse.*

JOHN LANDGRAF

Sharing God's Love with Others

Whether it's family, friends, associates, schoolmates, or total strangers, interacting with others is one of the most important things we do. We develop and live our lives in connection with others, especially through the friendships and relationships we form. The more we share God's love with other people, even in the smallest of ways, the more friendships and relationships we will have, and the more meaningful they will be.

If needed, this is an area of your life that you can improve, and significantly so, if you make a sincere choice to do so. It may not come easily, but it's one of the most worthwhile things you can do for yourself. The main ingredient in good relationships is your choice to treat others in an honest and positive way. Simply stated, the nicer you are to other people, the better and more enjoyable your life will be.

God will help you become a kinder and more helpful individual if you decide to make that one of your life's objectives. Your Spirit of Goodness is with you now, but you have to make choices that allow you to utilize the motivations and directions it provides. Although God and your Spirit of Goodness remain with you no matter what, you have to recognize that you either accept their guidance or block their influence with the choices you make.

There is probably nothing else you can do that will improve your life as much as your decision to share God's love and your goodness with others. Yes, money, education, good luck, and a few other things can make favorable impacts on your life. But none of these will make your life as enjoyable as consistently being kind and helpful to others.

Treat everyone with politeness and kindness,
not because they are nice,
but because you are.

ROY T. BENNETT

Example 11

A LOVE AND GOODNESS STORY
Suzanne Makes a Difference

Sometimes God calls us to do more than simply give a homeless person a little money. In this case, Suzanne, a restaurant owner, took a chance and offered Steven, a homeless man with a checkered past, the opportunity to restart his life. Here's the story about Steven.

A baggy-clothed homeless man who lived on the street begging for change got more than he bargained for when he strolled into Suzanne's cafe. Instead of turning the man away, the owner of the Sunshine Cafe asked him, "Why don't you have a job?"

Bowing his head to avoid eye contact, the man named Steven replied, "Well, I have a prison record and no one wants to hire me because of that. So, I've had to turn to the streets and get money the only way I know how, by stealing or begging for it."

Despite hitting a rough patch in her business, Suzanne made a decision. "You want a job? Then I have one for you." She asked him if he wanted to wash dishes for the day.

With a big grin, the man gladly accepted her offer. "I'll do anything for food."

As Steven finished washing his hands and tied an apron around his waist, Suzanne offered him a sandwich. Before eating, he wrapped half the meal in foil, ran outside, and gave it to a homeless woman waiting out on the street.

"That really touched me," Suzanne recalled.

After putting in two hours of work—the number of hours Suzanne could afford to pay him—Steven was on his way. The next day, he returned. For the next two weeks, he was on time for his two-hour shift. Suzanne then offered to make his position permanent.

Suzanne shared Steven's story on Facebook to encourage others to give strangers a shot. The post was shared more than 30,000 times and received more than 1,500 comments.

"We need more people like this," one person commented. "We are all human; we make mistakes."

"All we need sometimes is a helping hand," another said.

Steven, who had been living on the streets since he was sixteen years old, still had a long way to go to turn his life around.

"It's going to be hard for him to let go of whatever addiction he has," Suzanne said. "I want to help him, but he needs to want to help himself."

As a life-building step, the pair decided to take 10 percent from his paycheck and set it aside so he could learn to save his money.

Suzanne explained, "I had plenty of people to help me make it to where I am today. They believed I could do it. People need to have someone who believes in them."

Suzanne gave Steven the opportunity to restart his life. She, in her own special way, shared her love and goodness with Steven, and it clearly is making a major difference in his life. I especially noted Suzanne's comment that we all need to have someone who believes in us no matter what. My bet is that Steven makes it this time, all because someone cared enough to make the choice to help and believe he can do it.

CHAPTER 12

INCREASING YOUR GOODNESS

Opening Thought

Here are two paragraphs from a letter I received from someone who reviewed an early draft of this book. Because it shows how increasing our goodness by helping others helps us as well, I decided to include her comments here for you to read:

> *I had been considering donating to one of those toy drives for kids but felt like I hadn't found the right one, as selfish as that may sound. After reading a draft of this book and being reminded of how we should take note of our interests, abilities, and feelings, I did.*

> *When I was little, my father was incarcerated, and I remember how difficult those holidays were. So, I did some research and ended up finding a toy drive specifically for children of incarcerated parents and ordered a few toys from their wish lists. It not only made me feel good to think of those children receiving something they wanted, but it also made me feel like I had a little more purpose to my life.*

Focusing on Goodness

If you want to improve your life and get more satisfaction from living, increasing the level of goodness coming from your life is an important objective to establish. The purpose of our lives is to help others in some way. God has given us special interests, abilities, and feelings to do exactly that. That's God's part. Our part is making the choices that allow us to use those God-given qualities to help others in some way.

Although we have a lot of help—specifically, God's love and our Spirit of Goodness working within us—it's still up to us to make good choices and put them into practice. Ultimately, the goodness coming from our lives depends on these two things: the choices we make and how diligent we are in putting them into practice.

We can do more good by being good
than in any other way.

ROWLAND HILL

Different Strokes for Different Folks

When we look around our towns and communities, we note vast differences in the amount of goodness we see coming from the lives of others. Some people we know are great examples of *living with goodness* and always seem to be doing good and helpful things for people. We also know individuals who seem to have little or no goodness in them because they seldom, if ever, reach out to help someone in any special way.

So, there are helpful folks and self-centered folks and quite a variety in between. In other words, our personal goodness deliveries vary greatly.

Why the Differences in Goodness Between Individuals?

Bottom line: Our choices determine the amount of goodness coming from our lives. The more we choose to do good things for others—help a friend through a rough spot, support a teammate's idea, introduce someone new to others at work or school, volunteer to tutor a child—the more goodness our life provides. Yes, God's love and our Spirit of Goodness are always with us, nudging us to do helpful things for others, but it depends on us and the choices we make to actually do good things for others.

Although the amount of goodness coming from someone's life may be small or nonexistent right now, there is *always* the potential for a significant increase. Even people who have made big mistakes—who have wronged their family or friends in some way—and even those who have lived their daily lives in self-centered ways have the opportunity to stop what they are doing and start to increase the level of goodness coming from their lives. That's because God and our Spirit of Goodness are always with us and ready to help us when we're ready to make choices to do good and positive things for others.

How Do You Increase the Goodness Coming from Your Life?

There are three basic ways you can increase the goodness coming from your life:

- *Through your choices*: The quality of your choices directly affects the level of goodness coming from your life. You hold the controls, so to speak. Through your choices, you're in charge of the role that goodness plays in your life as well as the amount of goodness you deliver to others while you are here. To improve or increase the goodness coming from your life, you have to improve the choices you make.

- *Through your actions*: While our choices define how we want to help, it is through our actions that our goodness translates into actual benefits to others. You live out your goodness not just by thinking about it, but by actually *doing* something to help someone. We can't store up our goodness. We have to use it to help others today, or today's opportunities for words and deeds of goodness are lost forever.

- *Through your life's purpose*: Each of us possesses a unique combination of interests, abilities, and feelings—our way of doing things. If we pay attention to them, these unique qualities help us determine our purpose or calling in life. Because our true purpose will always have something to do with helping others, we enhance our life's opportunity for the delivery of goodness as we work to confirm and fulfill the purpose God has for our lives.

Will Your Goodness Be Challenged?

There will always be people who will influence you to put your goodness work aside and have some fun in life. However, as most of us recognize, a meaningful life is about more than just having fun. It's also about achieving a level of satisfaction that comes from living in a good and proper way. Real satisfaction comes from using your love and goodness to help others.

You'll most certainly encounter people whose suggestions, if followed, will diminish the amount of goodness coming from your life, but you can keep yourself from being a victim of such influences. You can remain an independent thinker, be the actual leader of your life, and make the choices that allow God and your Spirit of Goodness to become increasingly important influences in your life.

> *The purpose of life is not to be happy, but to matter,*
> *to be productive, to be useful, to have it make*
> *some difference that you have lived at all.*

LEO ROSTEN

The Need for More Goodness in This World

There are at least three important sources of goodness that need to be performing well to improve the circumstances we're experiencing in the world today:

- *From our people*: It may not be a nice thing to say that our country, and the world for that matter, has too many fools in it. However, it's true, and based on what I see, the number of fools is increasing rapidly. The number of shootings, store-grabs, killings, and other law-breaking events—as well as the number of people who treat others indifferently—seems to be increasing each day.

- *From our leaders*: We have world leaders, politicians, and other officials who are failing to lead with goodness in many places in the world today. I'm not certain what it would take to get these individuals—all of whom have special responsibilities to lead people in good and proper directions—to listen more closely to God and their Spirit of Goodness and use goodness as a factor in their decisions. However, if our citizens are going to start delivering more goodness from their daily lives, the leaders in this world have to set the example for others to follow.

- *From you and me*: One, God's love is at work within us. Two, our Spirit of Goodness is working within to motivate us to respond positively to God's love. And three, most of us are free to make choices that define how we live our lives. So, it appears we have everything we need—and more—to live a life where we can show concern for others and, whenever we can, reach out to help someone in some special way. The people in this world need to come together under the banner of goodness, work together to help each other, especially those in need, and commit to making the world a better place for everyone.

Peace among the nations, like happiness
for the individual, is not an end, but a byproduct
that comes when you live right.

EDWARD E. GRIGGS

You Ask: How Do I Spread More Goodness?

The answer, in my view, is straightforward. You make a special effort to take notice of God's love signals guiding your life in some way. You may not have paid much attention to these signals in the past, but doing so now—and doing your best to follow where they lead you to go—will improve not only your life, but equally important, the lives of others as well.

When you open yourself to being receptive to God in this way, your Spirit of Goodness will also nudge you to take action through your words and deeds to do the good and helpful things God is signaling you to do.

This is not some mystery to solve over a period of time or a series of steps you must complete to gear yourself for goodness. It's a choice you can make today to respond to God's love signals in positive ways. Recognized or not, God's love signals are working within you and your life right now. To complete the connection, you have to pay attention to the signals that God provides and then do the helpful things you are being led to do.

We've all had good, bad, and indifferent moments in our lives. Nevertheless, the objective of life is to maximize the good moments and minimize the other two. Frankly, we need some help to do this. That's the importance of recognizing that God has a presence in our lives. God is our connection to goodness and helps us make decisions about the kind of life we want to have. Ultimately, we make the choices that define our lives, but God is with us and will help us maximize our goodness if we are willing to let God do so.

*From the beginning I had a sense of destiny, as though
my life was assigned to me by fate and had to be fulfilled.
This gave me an inner security, and though I could never
prove it to myself, it proved itself to me. I did not have
this certainty; it had me. Nobody could rob me of
the conviction that it was enjoined upon me to do what
God wanted and not what I wanted. That gave me the
strength to go my own way. Often I had the feeling that
in all decisive matters, I was no longer among people
but was alone with God.*

CARL G. JUNG

Goodness Can Create Miraculous Moments

We typically think of miracles as move-a-mountain events in which an almost unbelievable happening takes place. Frankly, I haven't seen any miracles like that. On the other hand, I have witnessed people doing wonderful and important things for others that, without question, created miraculous moments in the lives of others. That's the type of event I'm referring to here, one in which one life touches another and makes a special difference in the lives of both individuals.

That said, I believe God's love and caring, working in our hearts, can help us create miraculous moments and even life-changing events. We may never consider that we could perform a miracle with what we say or do when we show special concern for someone. But how we treat someone, especially someone working through a difficult time in their life, can turn out to be a miraculous moment indeed.

It could be a telephone call to check on someone who is ill or facing a particular challenge in their life. It could be the delivery of an evening meal to the older couple who are not able to go out anymore. It could be some financial assistance to a destitute family having trouble paying their rent. The list of goodness possibilities goes on and on.

You are potentially a lot more important than you may have ever realized. There are a lot of special moments you can create if you choose to spend more of your time sharing your love and goodness with others. Regardless of your past or current circumstances, you can make a difference in the lives of others if you make the choice to do so.

Only a life lived for others is a life worthwhile.

ALBERT EINSTEIN

Example 12

A LOVE AND GOODNESS STORY

A Very Special Hardware Guy

We can definitely use more love and goodness in the marketplace these days, as customer service is not what it used to be. However, Joe the hardware man is an exceptional person and seems to take a personal interest in all his customers. The encounter with Joe described below reflects an actual experience my wife and I had just a few weeks ago.

I recently fell off a stool while replacing a light bulb in our kitchen. In an effort to break my fall, I grabbed for the handle on one of the kitchen drawers. Well, I ended up flat on my back on the kitchen floor, feeling a bit older, with the drawer handle in my hand. I had broken off the screws that secured it to the drawer.

A few days later, we went to the hardware store to find some new screws to reattach the handle to the drawer. Joe, who waited on my wife and me, tried a half dozen screws or more without any luck. He then informed us, "I think you stripped the threads inside the handle, so none of these are going to work."

Most people would have stopped right there, but not Joe.

Instead, he said, "Come with me" and took us to the small workshop in the back of the store. He went into the shop and worked diligently for over twenty minutes. When he came out, he advised us that he had rethreaded the handle and suggested we go back to the screw bin and try the screws again. This time, they worked perfectly.

Joe put four screws into a small plastic bag and wrote out the ticket: $1.56. A dollar fifty-six for all the work he'd done? Unbelievable, especially in today's economy. Obviously, we thanked him profusely and offered to pay more, but Joe simply said, "I'm glad I could help."

They don't make many people like Joe anymore. What a great guy!

This story shows the importance of sharing everyday love and goodness when we encounter someone in need. An important part of a meaningful life is to look out for one another as we go about our routines each day.

Clearly, Joe is an extraordinary man who showed a sincere interest in us and the problem we were trying to solve. No question, we need more people like Joe, not only at the hardware store but also throughout the world today. Thanks again, Joe, not only for your help that day, but also for being a love and goodness example that we all should follow.

CHAPTER 13

MANAGING YOUR LIFE

Opening Thought

Granted, there are some things in life we can't control. However, there are important things we can control but often fail to manage or improve as we should. This chapter reminds us of some critical factors that should be considered in managing and shaping our lives. It takes some insightful work on our part to effectively manage our thoughts, words, and deeds, but virtually every one of us can improve our management of these three things.

> *The thought manifests as the word,*
> *the word manifests as the deed,*
> *the deed develops into habit,*
> *and habit hardens into character.*
> *So watch the thought and its ways with care*
> *and let it spring from love, born out of concern for all beings.*

GAUTAMA BUDDHA

Your Most Important Task

When we are youngsters, our parents provide the rules and make many of our choices for us. But somewhere along the way, typically when we turn twelve or thirteen, we begin to take the driver's seat and start making many of the choices that define our lives. Soon after, we take full control. How our life works out from that point on—and how much love and goodness it imparts—is left primarily to us and the choices we make.

Some of our choices are significant: the career or role we choose in life, whom we marry, and how we take care of ourselves. In addition, we make many smaller choices every day: the clothes we wear, the way we conduct ourselves around others, and how we spend our free time are but a few such examples. The point is this: *You are in charge of your life, and you manage your life through the choices—large and small—that you make each day.*

Start with Those Love Signals

Paying attention to God's love signals at work within you and responding to the guidance that God provides will help you—more than anything—to perform well in all areas of life management. God will influence your life in very special ways if you pay attention to the signals that God provides. However, it takes a willingness to listen to your heart speaking to you and then an ability to decode the feelings God has created within you to determine how God is directing your life. One thing is for sure: God wants you to do good and helpful things for yourself, and equally important, for others. God will help you do exactly that if you make a sincere effort to follow where God is leading you to go.

Create a Management List

Never underestimate the importance of your life management responsibilities. How well you perform them determines what you will ultimately accomplish with your life. Therefore, it's not only help-ful but crucial to have some predetermined guidelines for making choices—a *life management list*, if you will, to help you make decisions.

There's no standard list to follow. Life management lists will vary by individual and how they choose to live their life. However, your list will most likely include both common sense guidelines for conduct-ing everyday life as well as some early thinking about unique goals or capabilities that you may have or want to develop. Such a list helps us think through key circumstances in life before they actually happen.

Your list might include the following:

- academic goals and objectives
- family duties and responsibilities
- how you will react when someone makes you mad
- friendships you need to develop (or curtail)
- research you want to do about something of interest
- exercise routines and food intake
- people you want to meet and talk to

And many more.

Take some time to think about your life management list, make some notes, and when you're ready, prepare an initial draft. No one gets these exactly right the first time, so expect to update and refine your list frequently in the early stages and from time to time after that.

Preparing such a list is extremely helpful in executing your life management duties because it allows you to plan ahead about what you will do, need to do, or should do in certain situations.

Consider the Goodness in Your Life

When you prepare your life management list, be sure to address the role of goodness in your life, and generally speaking, what you will do when you feel God's love signals at work within you, motivating you to say or do something helpful for someone. How will you react when you see someone in a circumstance or situation that you could help alleviate? What specific actions will you take to be a nicer and more caring individual? Typically, we don't consider "managing goodness" to be something to include on our to-do list, but clearly we can raise our awareness of the need for sharing our goodness with others—and help ourselves be better people—by placing "how we can help others" on our list.

> *You can preach a better sermon*
> *with your life than with your lips.*

OLIVER GOLDSMITH

Yes, it's great to have fun and enjoy life. But if you overlook the need for love and goodness and the roles they play in helping you create and maintain a meaningful life, at some point you are likely to be disappointed.

Keep These Points in Mind

Let me quickly say that these are my views and beliefs. You will have to decide if they are yours as well. However, here are four points that helped me understand the relationship between God's love and our goodness and the role they play in the management of our lives:

- *God is with us no matter what*: It's not a stretch for me to believe that our feelings of love and concern are really God's love signals at work within us and through us in the world. In other words, we are here to take care of each other, and our feelings of love and concern are, in effect, God motivating us to do so.

- *God has instilled a Spirit of Goodness in each of us*: This Spirit of Goodness helps motivate us to use our lives for the benefit of others. Some have referred to this presence as our conscience, but I see it as much more than that. Our conscience works after the fact. Our Spirit of Goodness, on the other hand, provides pre-event directional signals concerning specific things we should do to help others. God gives us our Spirit of Goodness, but it's left to us to develop it within our lives.

- *Sharing our goodness with others is a fundamental need in life*: We all have feelings of love and concern for others that, in turn, can stimulate the goodness coming from our lives. We help or hinder these feelings through the choices we make, but these feelings reside in everyone regardless of our past or present circumstances. What many of us fail to recognize is that we have a fundamental life management need to share our goodness with others. It's the single most important factor (not money or material success) in determining whether we live a meaningful life or not.

- *Our lives have a special purpose given to us by God*: One other point ties all of this together for me: Each of us has special interests, abilities, and feelings that point us to our intended purpose or calling in life. But much more than that, I can readily see that this is the way God works in the world: through love and goodness delivered by individuals like you and me. Therefore, one of our most important life management activities is to work diligently to determine our life's purpose and what God is calling us to do.

Test via Thoughts, Words, and Deeds

You can "test" sharing goodness and determine for yourself if increasing the level of goodness you display will help you live a better and more meaningful life. If you decide to test it out, it's helpful to think about sharing goodness within the three areas of your life you control the most: the ideas of goodness that are contained in your *thoughts*, the goodness you convey in your *words*, and the goodness delivered in your *deeds*.

The more goodness you incorporate into your *thoughts*, the better your attitude will be toward others. The more that goodness is reflected in your *words*, the more enjoyable your communications and relationships with others will be. And, of course, the more goodness you provide through your *deeds*, the more you will feel that your life counts for something and that you have actually made a difference in someone else's life.

> *I was in darkness, but I took three steps and*
> *found myself in paradise.*
> *The first step was a good thought;*
> *the second, a good word;*
> *and the third, a good deed.*

FRIEDRICH NIETZCHE

As you think about managing your life in more effective ways, remember that there are three main areas of life where we need to manage the level of goodness our lives impart:

- *Our thoughts*: We can find it next to impossible to control our thoughts. For the most part, they just happen. And we can't simply change a bad thought into a good one. It's not that easy. So, as you work on including more goodness in your thoughts, don't expect to change your thinking outright. Instead, work on introducing more good thoughts into your thinking. For example, instead of thinking about why you dislike Mary so much, think about one good quality she has or one good thing she has done. The more you look for good things in others and think good things about them, the better your thoughts will become.

- *Our words*: You'll have to agree that it is much better to say something nice or positive than otherwise. So, in your efforts to introduce more goodness into your words, simply look for more opportunities to compliment people. It has to be sincere, but an unexpected compliment makes both the recipient and you feel good. You can make someone feel special by simply saying, "Thanks very much! You did a great job. I appreciate the help." This "say something nice" attitude applies to every text message we send as well.

- *Our deeds*: Our typical reaction when we become aware of someone in need is to leave such circumstances to someone else to handle. "It's not my responsibility!" is the rather poor reasoning that frequently steers us around such moments in our lives. But wait a minute . . . this is why you're here: to use your life to help others in your own special way. One of the greatest feelings and experiences you will ever have is to make a positive difference in someone else's life. When you allow your Spirit of Goodness to work through you in this way, I can promise you that it will result in a feeling you'll never forget.

> *We live in deeds, not years; in thoughts, not breaths;*
> *in feelings, not in figures on a dial.*
> *We should count time by heart-throbs. He most lives*
> *who thinks most, feels the noblest, acts the best.*
>
> PHILIP JAMES BAILEY

As the quote above conveys, some action on our part is required for goodness to actually make its way from us into this world and into the lives of others. We can think good thoughts, and that's always important, but until we actually *say* or *do* something good that touches another person's life, our good thought—and the goodness it might convey—stays at home within us.

> *The smallest good deed is better than*
> *the grandest good intention.*
>
> JACQUES JOSEPH DUGUET

Consider These Fundamental Factors

Life never works out favorably on its own. We have to manage our lives with the choices we make each day. The final result of our life and what we accomplish with it is determined, to a great extent, by three crucial factors:

- *How we treat/help other people*: So important but overlooked by many of us is the simplest of things: being nice to others and treating the people we come in contact with each day, physically or electronically, with respect and kindness. Every one of us can score a "10" in this area of our life if we make a special effort to sincerely be nice to others.

- *The choices we make each day*: Near the end of each day, stop and think about the choices, especially the more important ones, you made or mentally worked on today. Be critical of yourself and give yourself an honest rating. One way you can learn or condition yourself to make better and more effective choices is to reflect on the quality of your most recent ones and determine if they were good choices or needed improvement.

- *The confirmation of our purpose or calling in life*: I didn't count the number of times I've referred to the importance of our "interests, abilities, and feelings" in this book, but it has been many, many times for sure. Don't overlook the value of working to decode what these God-given qualities are saying to you. You are being called to fill a special role, so work especially hard to determine what it is.

To be what we are,
and to become what we are capable of becoming,
is the objective of life.

ROBERT LOUIS STEVENSON

Example 13

A LOVE AND GOODNESS STORY

George's Happy Place

George is a great example of the importance of volunteers in society today. Although older and retired, George pitched in to help restore the landscaping in a large cemetery that had been neglected for years. His choice to help motivated others to pitch in as well.

Shadow Wood Cemetery was filled with weeds and overgrown grass, hiding all the headstones. When the cemetery came under new management, volunteers chipped in to help with restoration. George, a seventy-nine-year-old retired gentleman, volunteered to use his chainsaw to help restore the beauty of the property.

He worked several mornings each week, chainsawing, pulling bush, and hauling logs. He had seen an article outlining the struggles of the cemetery that motivated him to volunteer his time in retirement (no doubt, a love signal). He said volunteering was his happy place. He truly loved doing it and planned to continue as long as his body would allow him to.

George talked about wanting to give back to those who were shortchanged. He ended up helping with several other cemeteries, cutting trees at all of them. He saved the companies managing these cemeteries thousands of dollars with his work.

George was recognized for his volunteer work as well as his enthusiasm for the project overall. A local news company wrote a story about him and his work and gave him money as a noted individual in their volunteer spotlight.

George immediately gave the money back to the cemetery. "I don't need it, but Shadow Wood does, so I'm giving it to them."

When asked, George explained, "I do it because I love doing it."

The importance of people like George often gets overlooked. But it's people like George who not only have an interest in seeing things get better but are also willing to do their part to help convert a need for improvement into reality. I bet most of the people buried in that cemetery are smiling now because of what George and his fellow volunteers have done.

CHAPTER 14

HERE I AM, GOD, SEND ME

Opening Thought

There's not much question that the quality of life is declining in America and in many places around the world. Hate and indifference seem to be increasing, while love and caring for one another are on the decline. As a result, God could use more boots on the ground to improve these circumstances and spread more *love* and *goodness* here and around the world.

It's time for people everywhere to put down their weapons of *hate* and *selfishness* and start working to make life a positive experience for people everywhere. Unfortunately, God can't do this alone. God needs you, me, and many others to join in this important work of improving the world and creating opportunities where all people—regardless of their race, gender, politics, or location—can be free to become the individuals that God intended them to be.

So, how will you use your life and the capabilities God has given you to make life better and more satisfying, not only for yourself, but also for others, wherever they may be?

We need a worldwide awakening of the public conscience,
a spiritual revival, a moral regeneration,
before there can be real peace.

To this end, we do not need new laws, but a new spirit.
We do not need a change in government, but a change
of the human heart.

WILLIAM J. H. BOETCKER

Activating Your Love and Goodness

As you consider becoming more active in God's *love* and *goodness* work, here are two important points to keep in mind:

- *When you help someone, you help the world*: One of the great satisfactions in life occurs when we know we've helped someone in a special way. Helping others is what *love* and *goodness* are all about. Helpful words and actions don't have to be big deals to be meaningful. The important thing is to show that you genuinely care about the other person, whether it's with a hug and a smile or meaningful financial support. Our helpful life improvement work may include sharing *love* and *goodness* with a friend, a family member, a schoolmate, a business associate, or a total stranger. It could involve a next-door neighbor or someone thousands of miles away. *Whenever and wherever you help someone and improve the life of one person, even in a small way, you improve the world as well.*

- *God will be your partner in this work*: Spreading *love* and *goodness* is a partnership with God. God, you, and your Spirit of Goodness are a team whose objective is to help people in special ways. Therefore, it is crucial to communicate with God about your activities. This can be done via simple, honest prayers at any time. You may not have talked with God that much in the past. But now, as you make helping others a key part of your life, as you actually experience helping others in various ways, and as you see potential opportunities where you could make a difference in someone's life, you will have a lot more to talk about with God. *God will respond to you via special feelings in your heart and through meaningful thoughts and ideas that you develop.*

If you make the choice that you want to assist in God's work to make life and living better for others, no formal joining activity is required. Just pause right where you are, turn to God in prayer, and along with anything else you might want to say or ask, offer this request: "Here I am, God, send me." In so doing, you'll become an active member of God's team and be on your way to the most important days of your life as you work to share your *love* and *goodness* with people both near and far.

You're Already Equipped

You are already equipped to help carry out God's work in the world. As such, God has provided you with four important things:

- *A life*: First of all, you've been given a life to live and the opportunity to use that life to make positive differences in the world and in the lives of others.
- *Special gifts*: Second, God has given you a unique set of interests, abilities, and feelings to utilize as you identify and live out your life's purpose while you are here.
- *God's love signals*: Third, God provides you with love signals and guidance to help you identify people and situations where you can use your life to make life better for others.
- *A Spirit of Goodness*: Fourth, God has instilled a Spirit of Goodness within you to motivate and stimulate you to say the words and do the things that help others in this world.

Yes, it will require an exceptional effort on your part to utilize these gifts in special ways. But that's why you're here—not to make a lot of money, not simply to have a great time, but to share your personal gifts and your goodness with others.

What you possess in the world
will be found at the day of your death to belong to others,
but who you are will be yours forever.

HENRY VAN DYKE

Here I Am, God, Send Me

No question, we need a major renewal in this world in which people turn to God and live their lives with a focus on increasing the level of *love* and *goodness* their lives impart. We may live in different countries, have different skin colors, speak different languages, have lots of personal problems, and even have been oppressed by misguided political leadership, but we can still bow our heads and say, "Here I am, God, send me."

- *Send me . . . to be kind and polite to people*: Yes, I come in contact with many people each day—in person, on the phone, and via text or email. Help me, God, to be exceptionally nice, caring, and helpful to people regardless of what they say or how they treat me.

- *Send me . . . to help someone in need in a special way*: Yes, I see people in my town and in other parts of the world who have special needs such as food, clothing, or a safe place to sleep. Help me, God, to use my creativity and resources to develop and provide assistance to many of them.

- *Send me . . . to focus on my purpose in life*: Yes, I know that I'm a unique individual with ideas and capabilities that could be used to improve the lives of others. Help me, God, to listen to my interests, abilities, and feelings, to confirm my purpose for being here, and to make choices that allow me to deliver *love* and *goodness* through that purpose to others.

- *Send me . . . to share love and goodness with as many as I can*: Yes, please forgive me for the selfish and thoughtless things I've done in the past. Help me, God, to develop the *love* and *goodness* that my life, supported by good and worthy choices, can deliver to many of the people I touch with my life each day or may ultimately reach in other places in this world.

- *Send me . . . to help make the world a better place for everyone*: Yes, I know that hunger, discrimination, and health issues continue to be problems throughout the world. Help me, God, to say and do things that will help such individuals so that they can find their purpose, and as a result, further spread *love* and *goodness* throughout the world.

There are hundreds of other things God and our Spirit of Goodness might lead us to do. We are unique individuals capable of improving the world in some special way. It's up to us to determine if we are willing to accept the challenge of making the world a better place for everyone.

> *Little progress can be made*
> *by merely attempting to repress evil.*
> *Our great hope lies in developing what is good.*

CALVIN COOLIDGE

We Need More *Love* and *Goodness* in This World

I include here what, undoubtedly, is the most optimistic hope or wish a person could have: *that the people in this world will somehow unite under the shared purpose of helping each other have better and more meaningful lives.* No more wars, no more fighting, no more killings, no more hunger, no more differences—just the universal recognition that God and our Spirit of Goodness are at work motivating and guiding each and every one of us to help each other and to use our lives to make a meaningful difference in the lives of one another.

The selfish ways many people live in this world today make no sense. People and countries are at odds with each other and failing to see the benefits of working together to make the world a better place for everyone. Such poor conduct will never lead us to a feeling of universal fulfillment and will only create more and greater differences in the years to come. If we continue as we are doing now, we will at some point destroy ourselves, with God looking on in disbelief.

> *The world must learn to work together,*
> *or finally it will not work at all.*

DWIGHT D. EISENHOWER

Love and *Goodness*: A Better Way

Instead, God and our Spirit of Goodness are with us and available to help each one of us live a better and more fulfilling life. We can work together to make the world a better place if we make the choice to do so.

Making the world a better place will take *each* of us choosing *love* and *goodness* to guide what we say and do each day. It will take *each* of us putting aside hate and eliminating inconsiderate words and actions as we interact with others each day. It will take *each* of us doing our part to help others, thus making the world a little better because we have lived in it. And it will take local, national, and world leaders recognizing and understanding the true benefits of sharing God's *love* and *goodness* with all people everywhere.

Sharing love and goodness creates the threads that connect people in the world together. Regardless of your nationality, what country you live in now, and even other beliefs you may have had, you are connected to your brothers and sisters throughout the world through the sharing of love and goodness with each other. God has created this one great family here on earth. We need to help each other be that family.

I Believe We'll Get There

I know it's a stretch, but I believe that the people in this world will eventually adopt love and goodness as a way of life and work together to make the world a better place for everyone. I believe this for three key reasons:

- *People have a need to share love and goodness with others*: Deep down, each and every one of us, regardless of where we live or what our circumstances are at this moment, has a basic desire to live a life that is effective, meaningful, and makes a difference. We all want to feel that our lives are important and that we accomplished something with them. Clearly, the best way to achieve this feeling of satisfaction from our living is by delivering our *love* and *goodness* to others.

- *People need to feel love and goodness coming from others*: We all want to feel that there are people, close to us and otherwise, who care about us and have a personal interest in helping us have a better and more meaningful life. Clearly, it is through *love* and *goodness* that such feelings are created and shared.

- *Sharing love and goodness is the best way to make the world better*: The delivery of *love* and *goodness by* people *to* people everywhere is the only way to improve lives and make the world a better place for everyone. You and I can make a positive difference in this world if we're willing to make sharing *love* and *goodness* a priority in our lives.

The opportunities for you and me to share our love and goodness with others are virtually unlimited. We have family members, friends, neighbors, business associates, schoolmates, casual acquaintances, and even strangers within our reach who need to experience the love and goodness that you and I can provide.

So, it's not a matter of the need for more love and goodness in this world—that's a given. It's a matter of you, me, and millions of others *making the choice* to share God's gifts through the *love* and *goodness* our lives provide to as many of our brothers and sisters as we possibly can.

> *Any person who wants to give up their own self-centeredness*
> *and put their life on God's side*
> *will be put to work and given the same reward*
> *that the greatest saint receives,*
> *namely, fellowship with God.*

JAMES A. PIKE

Improving Lives, Improving the World

God's primary objective, as I believe it to be, is to make the world a better place for everyone by motivating us not only to improve our own lives, but equally important, to improve the lives of others. The world needs you, me, and millions of others to work with God to help people in important and needed ways. Unfortunately, not enough of us are fulfilling our responsibilities in this regard, and as a result, many lives in this world are getting worse, not better.

So, how will you know that God can make a real difference in your life? By doing the things that make positive differences in the lives of others. You will not only know it when you do such things, but you will also have living proof—yourself—that God can make a positive difference in your life, in the lives of others, and if enough people sign up to share their love and goodness with others, throughout the world.

> *To have lived so as to look back with pleasure*
> *on our past life is to live twice.*

MARTIAL

Example 14

A LOVE AND GOODNESS STORY

Sometimes, a Favor Is Returned

No, we should never reach out to help someone expecting a favor in return. Our love and goodness should be extended to others without the expectation of a "return payment" in any way. However, there are times when a favor, possibly due to God being at work in our lives, works out to produce unexpected benefits for someone who reached out to help someone in need. Such was the case of Victor.

Victor, sixty-one, and his wife were driving to Indiana when they saw two young women pulled over on the side of the interstate with a flat tire. Victor pulled over as well and helped them change the tire before continuing on his way. Unfortunately, a few miles later, while driving, Victor suffered a heart attack and, with his wife's assistance, pulled their car to a stop on the shoulder.

A few seconds later, Sara, one of the women Victor had just helped, saw him pull over, and she stopped as well. When Victor's wife told Sara what was happening, Sara jumped into action. It just so happened that she was a certified nursing assistant. She performed CPR on Victor until first responders arrived and were able to take him to the hospital. She had, in effect, repaid the man who had helped change her tire by saving his life.

Prior to his release, Sara visited Victor in the hospital. Hospital staff and first responders also attended the reunion in Victor's room at the hospital. Victor once again expressed his gratitude to Sara. Victor and Sara hugged, then both started crying.

After his release from the hospital, Victor still seemed taken aback by being the center of all the attention. "I'm just an old Joe, you know," he said. "To have so much attention and so many people to care for me was just overwhelming. I always like to be the caregiver. I'm not used to being taken care of."

I'm not qualified to say that God orchestrated these circumstances, but I can clearly see that love and goodness had everything to do with it. Not only did Victor respond with love and goodness when he saw the problem the two women were having, but I believe that love and goodness were afoot again when Sara became concerned about seeing Victor's car pulled over by the side of the road.

And somewhere along the way, it was those God-sponsored qualities (gifts) that had led Sara to become a nurse in the first place. We may not be able to explain God's role in all of this, but it's easy to see the benefits that occurred from the love and goodness of the people involved.

CHAPTER 15

RECONNECTING
OUR DIVIDED WORLD

Opening Thought

As I conclude the writing of this book, war is going on between Russia and Ukraine and between Israel and Hamas. Over six hundred thousand people have been killed and over twice that number wounded in these two wars. Some online research identifies fifty-six armed conflicts going on in the world as I write this, the most since World War II. These include terrorist insurgencies, civil wars, drug wars, wars between countries, and ethnic violence.

In addition to these major conflicts, crimes and killings are increasing at a rapid rate in almost every major city and country in the world. Also notable is that public protests and political differences occupy an increasing portion of the national news in most countries each day.

You'd think we'd be smart enough not to let all of this happen and instead would find ways to communicate and work together to make life better for *everyone everywhere*. But after thousands of years of worldwide development, that level of cooperation hasn't happened. In fact, things are getting worse, and we are continuing to head in the wrong direction.

We have just enough religion to make us hate,
but not enough to make us love one another.

JONATHAN SWIFT

Disconnected in Our Religious Beliefs

It is estimated that there are over four thousand religions worldwide. The largest of these are Christianity, Judaism, Islam, Buddhism, and Hinduism. Included in this estimate are over three hundred religions in the United States. While similarities exist between some of these groups, there are thousands of organized views about God and how God works in the world.

Organized religions, especially the larger ones, have well-defined belief statements as well as related publications that explain what the church or group corporately believes. In addition, most members and regular attendees have a number of personal beliefs that they've developed from various religious experiences or through interactions with family and others over the years. We may also have a few special beliefs about life and living that we've developed from our life experiences and that have become part of our group of beliefs. Therefore, our religious beliefs tend to come from a combination of sources, and some of our beliefs are stronger than others.

However, regardless of where your beliefs come from, the important question is this: *How do your beliefs influence the way you live your life?* It's one thing to have your religious beliefs, but it's so much more if those beliefs motivate you to do good and positive things with your life. In other words, it's not just what you <u>believe</u>, but also what you <u>do</u> with your life as a result of those beliefs that really counts.

Add the "Un-Churched" Folks

The number of views and beliefs about God expands even further when you consider the millions of individuals who are not members or participants in any organized church or religious group. According to a recent Gallup poll, just over 50 percent of the US population indicates that they have no church membership. Therefore, there are millions of "unchurched" individuals who have their own views of God or no view at all.

This means there are thousands of organized religions and millions of independent views about God. In addition, there are lots of us who, although active in our church or religious group, remain "in neutral" as far as working to confirm what we actually believe about God and how God works in the lives of people. Many of us say we believe, but in fact do little to make a helpful difference in the lives of other people.

It's a difficult thing to admit, but given all the needs, problems, and conflicts in this world today, religions worldwide, organized and otherwise, are not making the impact for a good and better world that they should be making. *Bottom line: We need more people who believe that God put them on this earth to make life better for others, whether a member of a church or not.*

Our Divided World

The point I'm trying to make is that we live in a very divided world, not only geographically, politically, and economically, but in our religious practices as well. We need to set our differences aside, focus less on the details of our organized religions, and work harder—*as human beings*—on how God's *love* and our *goodness* can help us have better lives and a better world.

This book was written to help you to take one step beyond your beliefs, not simply to confirm your personal beliefs, but more importantly, to help you identify what you will *do* as a result of what you believe. How will your beliefs lead you to be a better person and to help others have better lives? What will your beliefs motivate you to actually *do* to make life better for others and the world a little better as well?

True religion is not a mere doctrine,
something that can be taught,
but is a way of life.
A life in community with God. It must be
experienced to be appreciated.
A life of service.
A living by giving and finding one's own happiness
by bringing happiness into the lives of others.

WILLIAM J. H. BOETCKER

Reconnecting Our Divided World

So, given the problems and situations we have throughout the world today, how can we ever reconnect our divided world? This would not only be a major undertaking, but also, worldwide love and goodness is something we have never worked collectively to achieve. But it can be done. In my view, we can make significant progress in this regard if people everywhere recognized and acknowledged the following four things.

#1. There Is a Need for Love and Goodness Throughout the World

I may be more than a bit naïve, as well as overly optimistic, but I believe we could move away from these worldwide problems if we had a set of love and goodness beliefs that were supported by all religions worldwide and that guided the lives of people everywhere. That set would include the following love and goodness beliefs:

- *God's love and our goodness are needed throughout the world*: God's love and our goodness need to be a part of everyone's lives, regardless of geographical location, political circumstances, or past beliefs.

- *Our choices determine if we follow God's influence and leadership or not*: Our dispensing of God's love and goodness to others depends on the choices we make as we encounter people during our lives each day. Our choices are so powerful that they define our lives and the level of goodness we impart.

- *People throughout the world can help each other*: God has given each of us a unique set of interests, abilities, and feelings that we should use to confirm our purpose and to help others have better lives. People in countries around the world could benefit immensely from sharing ideas, resources, and an abundance of love and goodness with each other.

- *God works primarily through people and depends on you, me, and others to deliver God's love and goodness throughout the world*: We have a crucial role in life—yes, each and every one of us—as it is through our individual lives that much of God's work in the world gets done.

The primary objective of individuals who choose to adopt these beliefs and join in this worldwide love and goodness work would be to encourage and guide participants to use their lives to help others have better and more meaningful lives. The ultimate goal would be to unite people throughout the world under one love and goodness banner motivating participants to work together to make the world a better place *for everyone*.

Our business is not only with eternity but with time,
to build up on earth the kingdom of God,
to enable people to live worthily and
not merely die in hope.

LORD TWEEDSMUIR

#2. God Has Equipped Us for This Work

God has gifted each of us with a unique set of interests, abilities, and feelings that are meant to be utilized to determine and carry out our purpose in life as electricians, abuse counselors, real estate agents, HR specialists, airline pilots, and in thousands of other ways. Whatever you have been called to do with your life, you will be much more effective if you make *love* and *goodness* an important part of it.

No formal sign-up process is required to become part of this special group of love and goodness supporters. You just have to raise your hand and prayerfully say to God, "Here I am, God, send me." Then look for ways to help others by sharing your love, abilities, and resources with them.

> *The greatest tragedy is not death,*
> *but a life without purpose.*

> RICK WARREN

#3. Doing Is as Important as Believing

Our lives leave trails of words, deeds, and accomplishments that develop over many years based on the choices we make each day. When we are no longer here, friends and family will think about us from time to time and reflect on the trail of words and deeds we left behind. The question is: What kind of trail will you leave? Leaving a trail of love and goodness is something that each of us should strive to achieve.

It seems to me that our religious beliefs would be somewhat meaningless if they didn't stimulate us to *do* something meaningful and worthwhile with our lives. What's the point of believing if it doesn't push us to live a better life?

Yes, the willingness of God to accept us as we are is a significant and wonderful thing. However, partnering with God to help others and actually working to make the world a better place seems to be even more important to me. May God bless you in a special way as you consider what you will actually *do* to make the world a little better because you were here.

True religion is the life we live,
not the creed we profess.

J. F. WRIGHT

#4. God Will Guide Us in This Work

Regardless of where we have been, what we have done, or what we may have believed in the past, God will support and guide us—both individually and collectively—as we do the work and share the goodness needed to make the world a better place for everyone.

- God will guide us as we reach out to people in our towns and cities and do helpful things, both large and small, to make their lives better in some way.

- God will be with us as we work to make each of our countries places where all people are loved and those in need are helped in meaningful ways.

- God will help us reach beyond our borders and boundaries to extend loving and helpful hands and provide needed resources to others in this world.

Love and goodness are needed throughout the world—in every country, in every town and city, and in every community and neighborhood. People everywhere need our helpful words and supporting deeds if we're going to make the world a good, happy, and beneficial place for all. Working together, we can reconnect our divided world and make it a better place for everyone.

It's Up to Us and the Choices We Make

It would be much easier if God would perform a major miracle and everyone everywhere would wake up tomorrow morning no longer living in fear and having all the food, shelter, and opportunities they needed to live a productive life. But God doesn't work that way. Instead, God works through people. Therefore, it will take you, me, and millions of others making the choices needed to work in good and positive ways to help others have meaningful and productive lives.

We can make the world a better place, and God will help us in very special ways. However, it will require people throughout the world to take steps toward worldwide love and goodness by making the choice to share their *love* and *goodness* with people where they live and work. We need more people whose lives reflect God's love signals working through them to help people and whose helpful words and deeds create *the additional goodness* this world so badly needs.

Will you be one of these helpful and caring people?

> *To have a free, peaceful, and prosperous world,*
> *we must be even stronger, especially in spiritual things.*
> *It is a belief in decency, justice, progress,*
> *and the value of individual liberty*
> *conferred on each of us by our Creator*
> *that will carry us through.*

DWIGHT D. EISENHOWER

Example 15

A LOVE AND GOODNESS STORY

Fueled by Faith

This is a wonderful example of how God will use us if we are willing to follow God's lead, even before we are fully aware of what God wants us to do. Dr. Tom Catena felt God's presence in his life during his younger years and made a commitment to do mission work before he knew exactly where God was leading him. As you will see, God and Dr. Catena teamed up to make major differences in the lives of many people.

After completing his studies at the Duke University School of Medicine and a stint in the US Navy, Tom Catena reconfirmed the commitment to mission work he had made in his younger years when he was uncertain exactly what his mission work would be. Now equipped with his medical degree, he made the decision to provide much-needed medical services in Africa.

Looking back, he said, "I thought I would spend a year or so doing mission medicine in Kenya and then come back and get on with things."

Twenty-five years later, Dr. Tom Catena is still helping people in Africa. After spending eight years in Kenya, he moved to the mountains of Sudan to help develop their medical services. He went in support of a Catholic bishop who was trying to build a hospital there.

When he arrived, he was immediately reminded of what he had been told: "If you think things are tough in Kenya, just wait until you see things in Sudan." It was apparent that life there was not going to be easy. At that time, the hospital was just under discussion, and there were only fifteen medical workers in an area that had over a million people.

Seventeen years later, and in spite of limited equipment and medical supplies, the Mother of Mercy Hospital has been established with over 270 trained medical workers to help the people there. Dr. Catena sees dozens of patients each day.

A fellow worker said, "Tom is the most committed person I know. He values every single patient he sees and works endlessly."

Dr. Catena said, "My faith has kept me here. I know that this is what God wanted me to do."

Wow! The world could certainly use several million more mission-minded people like Dr. Catena. Clearly, God waited for him to get his medical degree and then guided him to deliver much-needed medical services to the people in both Kenya and Sudan. Dr. Catena is living proof that it takes more than just believing *to improve lives and make the world a better place. It takes* doing *something and being willing to respond favorably when God calls us to the task of spreading goodness with the life that has been given to us.*

CLOSING WORDS

I hope the points, beliefs, and feelings shared in this book have reso-nated with you in some way. The world needs its people to come together and follow God's love signals as we all work to live better and more helpful lives. We need to say and do more things that help our brothers and sisters, regardless of who they are or where they might be. As you reconfirm your efforts to live in a positive and productive way, please remain mindful of the two most important things in your life: God's love and your goodness.

God's Love

I believe that God loves us unconditionally and that God guides our lives through the love signals we feel in our hearts. Such love signals direct us to people we care deeply about, to projects, vocations, and life roles we feel led to pursue, and to individuals who need help in some way. God's love signals help us develop our lives in meaningful ways.

It's up to us to take note of the love signals that God provides and to respond to them in what we say and do each day. There are lots of people who need the love and caring that you and I can provide. God needs us and many others to help in specific ways to make life better and improve the circumstances of others. By responding to God's love signals in positive ways, we form a partnership with God in which we work together to improve individual lives and make the world a better place.

Your Goodness

Regardless of our past, each of us has a Spirit of Goodness, given to us by God, that nudges us to respond favorably to God's love signals and to utilize the personal gifts and qualities that God has given us. However, our choices determine the amount of goodness our life provides. If you are a good and helpful person, it's because you are making the choices required to live your life that way. If you're not sharing your goodness with others, your choices are to blame. God gives us a start toward goodness and leads us in that direction, but it is left to us and our choices to determine the level of goodness our life provides.

There are no greater choices in life than the ones that define how you will help God help others and make the world a little better because you are here. It's not just believing in helping others that counts, but what you actually *say* and *do* to improve someone's life that in turn makes your life a more meaningful one. May God guide you in a special way as you work to determine how your words and deeds will make others' lives better and improve the world in some way.

> *What our deepest self craves is not mere enjoyment,*
> *but some supreme purpose that will enlist all our powers*
> *and give unity and direction to our lives.*

HENRY J. GOLDING

Don't Leave God Out of Your Life

You may not understand everything about God. You might not know exactly what God wants you to do with your life. You may have more questions than answers. However . . .

- . . . that doesn't mean you can't make the choice to partner with God now and work to develop a stronger relationship with God over time.

- . . . that doesn't mean you can't start paying closer attention to God's love signals when they enter your life and responding to them as best you can.

- . . . that doesn't mean you can't work to make better choices, to be nicer to people, to help people more, and to be a good person.

So, whatever you decide to do with your life, don't leave God out of it. No matter who you are or what you have or haven't done, your life will be so much better with God in it. Your current belief status doesn't matter; your partnership with God will help you improve it.

- *If you happen to be a nonbeliever*, maybe it's because you have never really listened for God's love signals within you and worked to determine how they are directing your life. Maybe it's because you have never considered yourself to be here to help God make life a little better for those with whom you come in contact each day. If so, working to live in a more helpful way will improve your nonbelief and help you see that God has a definite purpose for you and your life.

- *If you have questions concerning your beliefs*, as many do, don't let that be the reason you fail to listen for God's love signals and work to understand how God is directing your life. Believing in God is not a simple achievement. You have to work at it and actually *say* and *do* helpful things for others in order to attain an understanding of both the *results you achieve* and the *feelings you have* when you help God improve the lives of other people.

- *If you are a believer and active church member*, don't leave God at the church and fail to pay attention to God's guidance the other six days of the week. Yes, it's important to be part of a church or group of believers who, like you, are working to live in partnership with God. But when the service or meeting is over, make sure you stay in touch with God throughout your week.

The unfortunate truth is that an increasing number of people are leaving God out of their lives. This is the reason we are experiencing a growing number of problems within our communities and cities and within countries throughout the world. However, God will guide us to better ways of living and help us to be better people if we make the choice to respond positively to the love signals that God provides.

Let God Be Your Guide

As I close out the book, I want to reemphasize one point that I made several times. We've made believing in God way too complicated when, in reality, partnering with God is one of the most logical and beneficial things we can do. Everyone in this world needs special guidance to live helpful and worthwhile lives. God's love signals provide that guidance. Through acts of goodness, our response to those love signals creates a partnership with God that helps us, as well as others, have better lives.

You may not understand many of the things that happened thousands of years ago. However, that's not a requirement to seek and experience God's guidance in your life *today*. To establish and maintain a partnership with God, I suggest you start doing three basic things:

- *Pay attention to God's love signals*: Start paying attention to the love signals God is already sending to you that guide your life in positive and caring ways.

- *Say and do good and helpful things*: Start *saying* and *doing* good and helpful things for others that God's love signals are motivating you to *say* and *do*.

- *Talk to God about living in a helpful way*: Start talking to God about the feelings you have from living in this good and helpful way and ask God for guidance in becoming the individual that God wants and needs you to be.

These are three straightforward and easily repeatable steps that will help you confirm and maintain your connection to God. God will always help you, but it's important for you to take a step toward God and ask for God's guidance as an indication of your desire for God's assistance in developing and managing your life.

It's important to remember that God loves all of us, without exception. God may be disappointed in some of the things we have done, especially when we've failed to reach out and help someone in need or made some terrible choice that took our lives in a bad direction. Nevertheless, God still loves us, forgives us, and will help us if we acknowledge the love signals that God sends and make a sincere effort to follow where they are leading us to go.

God's Calling for You and Me

Merriam-Webster defines a calling as "a strong inner impulse toward a particular course of action especially when accompanied by divine influence." We all have a calling from God concerning how we should live. As such, each of us has a divine reason for being here. God's love signals help us to understand that reason and how we should develop it within our lives.

However, many of us devote our lives to various activities without ever acknowledging the calling God has for us. Others have felt such a calling but, for a variety of reasons, have never reached the point of conviction to begin viewing their lives as a partnership with God devoted to making people's lives better in some way.

I want to leave you with a challenge to think carefully about what you have felt or are feeling now about God's intentions for your life.

Is there something you feel God is calling you to do? Are there meaningful adjustments that you feel God wants you to make in the way you are living? I urge you to think carefully about how God is calling you as you consider your life and how it should be lived.

I believe that God calls each of us in three basic ways:

- *God calls us to be nice and kind*: We are called by God to be nice people and to be considerate of the people we come in contact with each day. We may not like or agree with everyone, but God calls us to treat others in respectful and courteous ways, regardless of how we feel. When we conduct ourselves in nice and kind ways, we not only have more friends, but we also accomplish so much more with our lives.

- *God calls us to be helpful*: We are called by God to be concerned about others, especially those in need, and to use our lives to help people have better and more enjoyable lives. We are called by God to improve other people's lives and to do our part to make the world a little better while we are here. It's important to note that when you help someone in a special way, you are actually sharing God's love with them.

- *God calls us to be ourselves*: God has given each of us a unique set of interests, abilities, and feelings that guide us to become teachers, parents, bankers, farmers, bakers, drivers, and millions of other vocations or roles that are needed to improve the world and help each other have better lives. There is a special mission inside each of us, and God's calling helps us to confirm that mission and to bring it into reality in our lives.

The Challenge for You and Me

The challenge for all of us is to manage our lives in such a way that we become the *loving, helpful,* and *unique* individuals God has intended and is leading us to be. God will help you accomplish all three of these objectives if you pay attention to God's love signals and make the choices required to follow where God is leading you to go.

Sharing your goodness with others is a prerequisite to developing and living a meaningful and effective life. Just being smart is not enough. Just being good-looking won't do it. Just being a hard worker won't get you there. You have to share your goodness and reach out to help others if you want to develop a special life.

The size of the goodness you share is not the important thing. What's key is that you help other people and show that you care about them. May God bless you and guide you in special ways as you manage your life and use your *goodness* to improve the lives of others, and in so doing, make the world a better place.

Most of us are familiar with this basic advice about life: *Do unto others as you would have others do unto you.* This recommendation not only emphasizes the *do* aspect of living our lives, but it also calls for our words and deeds to be consistent with the way we would like others to treat us. This is great advice for living, and if we pay attention to God's love signals, God will help us *do* exactly that.

Thinking well is wise;
planning well, even wiser;
doing well the wisest and best of all.

PERSIAN PROVERB

God Will Help You Become a Better Version of Yourself

It's difficult these days to develop our lives in good, independent, and positive ways. That's because our lives are influenced by so much information, by so many people, and in so many ways. Some of these influences are helpful, but many are not.

Despite these influences, there is a unique individual within each of us who has a special set of interests, abilities, and feelings and the hope to do something meaningful with their life. To develop these qualities, as well as fulfill the personal expectations we have for our lives, each of us must work our way through the influences we encounter, utilizing the good ones while insulating ourselves from the bad.

We all need help to develop our lives effectively. We need help to navigate our way through the influences we experience and to find the motivation to use our lives to help others in special ways. Your partnership with God and the love signals that God provides will help you work your way through this influential world, help you become a better person, and help you become the individual you were always intended to be. *The fact that your relationship with God will help you become a better version of yourself may be the most important point in this whole book.*

> *Before I can tell my life what I want it to do,*
> *I must listen to my life telling me who I am.*
> *This does not come from a voice "out there"*
> *calling me to become something I am not.*
> *It comes from a voice "in here" calling me*
> *to be the person I was born to be,*
> *to fulfill the original selfhood given to me by God.*

PARKER PALMER

TALKING WITH GOD

God will help you lead a better life if you talk with God about your life and what you are working to accomplish with it. God will help you think things through and evaluate various alternatives you may have. God will help you treat others with kindness and respect. Frequent, even short, conversations with God will help you develop and live a more meaningful life. If you need a little assistance in this regard, please use the prayer below, or simply select one of its paragraphs and talk to God about it.

A Love and Goodness Prayer

God, please help me to be a good person.

Help me to take note when your love signals
have entered my life and to make the choices needed
to follow where those signals are leading me to go.

Please keep my Spirit of Goodness active and
motivating me to do helpful and worthwhile
things for others.

Please help me focus on the interests, abilities,
and feelings you have given me.

Help me to develop these qualities as I work to identify and fulfill the purpose You have for my life.

Help me to always remain mindful of the needs of others and to use my life to create more goodness in the world through what I say and do each day.

Amen.

THANK YOU!

Dear Reader,

Thank you for traveling with me through this book and allowing me to share my beliefs and feelings with you. My hope is that I've helped you think about the goodness coming from your life. Partnering with God to make others' lives better is an opportunity available to everyone. There is something very special about developing the understanding that God is working through you to improve another person's life.

Back to our opening question: How does God work in the world? I believe God works through people like you and me to make others' lives better in many different ways. It is because of God working through our lives that hungry people are fed, sick people are healed, people in need are assisted, and others are loved in special ways. Subject to the choices we make, you and I are God's delivery system as we use our lives to make life better for others.

If you need further evidence, I urge you to make the choice to help a few people in special ways and then talk to God about how living in this helpful way makes you feel. I believe it's this <u>doing</u> part, not just the <u>believing</u> part, of our connection to God that is so important. Doing helpful things makes life better for others, improves our own lives, and strengthens our relationship with God as well.

May God bless you in a special way as you work to live your life in this helpful way.

—Michael Nelson

ABOUT THE AUTHOR

Michael L. Nelson

Michael graduated from the University of Mississippi and worked for IBM in Memphis, Tennessee, for the first ten years of his business career. He went on to become a partner in a technology-related leasing company and to serve as the president of a large technology services organization in Chicago, Illinois. In addition, Michael served on the board of a Mid-South bank for over ten years.

Michael and his wife, Betty, have two grown children, both with MBAs and very successful in their own right. In addition, they have three wonderful grandchildren, all with college degrees and now making some good choices of their own.

Michael has written three other books: *Good Choices Good Life*, *Living by Choice*, and *Life and Choices*. All are currently available on Amazon.

Michael has come to strongly believe that God works primarily through people. The most important spiritual influences in our lives, he believes, are provided by God via love signals in our hearts and are supported by our God-given Spirit of Goodness, which motivates us and helps us respond to the love signals that God provides.

As he has thought about God's presence over the years, he has come to realize the almost unbelievable importance of our choices. Our choices provide a pathway for us to follow the love signals provided by God and to help others in some special way.

AUTHOR WEBSITE

MichaelsBooks.com

BOOKS BY
MICHAEL L. NELSON

Good Choices Good Life

BECOMING THE PERSON YOU WERE INTENDED TO BE

Living by Choice

MAKING THE DECISIONS THAT DEFINE YOUR LIFE

Life and Choices

A PERSONAL DEVELOPMENT GUIDE

(Available on Amazon)

www.ingramcontent.com/pod-product-compliance
Lightning Source LLC
Chambersburg PA
CBHW021150130626
46554CB00005B/1747